# Praise for *Where Is God?*

"John Townsend brings a unique combination of insight from years of counseling and personal coaching, wedded with a passion for God and an effective working knowledge of the Scriptures. John addresses probably the single most troubling question of any age with unique insight and theological sensitivity. This book will really help those asking, 'Where is God when I really need Him?'"

—MARK L. BAILEY, PHD
President, Dallas Theological Seminary

"From the dawn of humanity we have cried out to God through the darkest night, 'Are you there? Do you see me?' In this rock-solid book, Dr. Townsend answers those questions, not with wishful thinking but with truth you can build your life on. This book is a gift to us in times like these."

— –SHEILA WALSH
Women of Faith® Speaker and Author, *Beautiful Things Happen When a Woman Trusts God*

"I am so glad that John has addressed this very real felt-need. He speaks out of experience, having helped many people find God in times of pain. I highly recommend this book."

—DR. HENRY CLOUD
Psychologist, Author, and Leadership Consultant

"This book is not about providing answers but rather experiencing a heartfelt relational connection to both God and man during life's darkest hours. A must-read for those who question God's love and care because of the painful things that have happened in life. This book will be required reading for the young women we reach through Mercy Ministries."

—NANCY ALCORN
Founder and President, Mercy Ministries International

"When adversity strikes and people are overcome with loss, pain, or trauma, the wish to be lifted out of misery is most evident. Regardless of one's connection to God, we all seem to muster up childlike faith when faced with the limits of ourselves, looking to God for relief and rescue. In *Where Is God?* Dr. John Townsend thoroughly and confidently walks us through this earnest question for those times when we need God the most and wonder if He notices our struggles and cares enough to show up. This vitally important book helps us draw close to and connect with God, who is very, very personal yet bigger than we can imagine."

—JILL HUBBARD, PhD
*New Life Live!* Cohost and Author, *The Secrets Women Keep*

"For new Christians and doubting believers, this is the best book—and John is the best author—to answer the most important question of anyone's life."

—STEVE ARTERBURN
Founder, Women of Faith® and New Life Ministries

"Have you noticed on your car's side-view mirror the words, *Objects may appear larger than they really are*? That's the way trials seem when they come upon us. Fortunately, you're holding a book, written by a good friend, that not only can put the challenges you're facing into proper perspective but also can help you see God's perspective on what's happening in your life. I recommend it for anyone ready to gain more hope and shrink fears and doubt."

—JOHN TRENT, PhD
President, StrongFamilies.com; Coauthor, *The Blessing*;
and Author, *The 2 Degree Difference*

# WHERE IS GOD?

# WHERE IS GOD?

## FINDING HIS PRESENCE, PURPOSE, AND POWER IN DIFFICULT TIMES

# DR. JOHN TOWNSEND

THOMAS NELSON
*Since 1798*

NASHVILLE   DALLAS   MEXICO CITY   RIO DE JANEIRO

Published in Nashville, Tennessee, by Thomas Nelson. Thomas Nelson is a registered trademark of Thomas Nelson, Inc.

Published in association with Yates & Yates, LLP, www.yates2.com.

Thomas Nelson, Inc., titles may be purchased in bulk for educational, business, fund-raising, or sales promotional use. For information, please e-mail SpecialMarkets@ThomasNelson.com.

Scripture quotations marked NKJV are taken from the New King James Version®. © 1982 by Thomas Nelson, Inc. Used by permission. All rights reserved.

Scripture quotations marked NASB are taken from the New American Standard Bible®. © The Lockman Foundation 1960, 1962, 1963, 1968, 1971, 1972, 1973, 1975, 1977. Used by permission.

Scripture quotations marked NLT are taken from the Holy Bible, New Living Translation. © 1996, 2004. Used by permission of Tyndale House Publishers, Inc., Wheaton, Illinois 60189. All rights reserved.

Scripture quotations marked NIV are taken from the Holy Bible: New International Version®. © 1973, 1978, 1984 by International Bible Society. Used by permission of Zondervan Publishing House. All rights reserved.

ISBN: 978-0-8499-4686-8 (IE)

**Library of Congress Cataloging-in-Publication Data**

Townsend, John Sims, 1952–
  Where is God? : finding His presence, purpose, and power in difficult times / John Townsend.
    p. cm.
  Includes bibliographical references.
  ISBN 978-0-7852-2919-3 (hardcover)
  1. Spirituality—Christianity. 2. God (Christianity)  I. Title.
  BV4501.3.T694 2009
  248.8'6—dc22                                                      2009034502

*Printed in the United States of America*

10 11 12 13 14 WC 8 7 6 5 4

This book is dedicated to everyone who has looked
to the sky in hard times, asking,

*Where is God?*

May you find Him and His care for you.

# CONTENTS

# ACKNOWLEDGMENTS

My thanks to the following people who were instrumental in the development of this book:

*Matt Baugher*, Publisher, Thomas Nelson, Inc. Thanks for coming up with the title and for all your structural feedback on the material. Your help and support came at the right time and in the right places.

*Sealy Yates* and *Jeana Ledbetter*, literary agents. You resourced, brought perspective, and provided encouragement through the process. Thanks yet again for everything.

*Kate Etue*, copy editor. The diligence and craft you brought to the content has helped this book to be a better experience for the reader.

*Liz Babyak, Dr. Keith Edwards,* and *Ariel Okamoto*. Thanks for the neurological research support and your competence in the field.

*Greg Campbell*. Your overviews and suggestions were very timely and had a significant and positive impact on the quality of the material.

*Dr. Jay Martin*. Thanks for your support in the conceptualization of what the book means on a deeper level.

*Cathy Evangelatos.* Your thoughts about how people's experiences matter helped make the material accessible to anyone who struggles.

*The Executive Men's Small Group* and *team members of the Leadership Coaching Program.* Again, your feedback and responses resulted in a much better book.

*My wife, Barbi, and our sons, Ricky and Benny.* Thanks for all the time you took, talking to me about the ideas here and helping me craft how they were written.

Finally, *all the theologians, philosophers, scientists, thinkers, believers, and writers who, through the centuries, have sought God and reflected deeply.* Your thoughts and writings have helped us all to find Him.

# INTRODUCTION
## WHERE IS GOD WHEN I NEED HIM?

The temperature on the glacier was relatively warm, and the air was still. At least it was warmer than I had thought it would be, hovering around 20 degrees Fahrenheit. I should have expected that though. It was January, the middle of the Antarctic summer. I was on a cross-country skiing excursion to the crest of the glacier. But wind and weather change quickly there, as I was soon to find out.

I had been planning to travel to Antarctica for years, having always been intrigued by the mysterious ice continent, population maybe four thousand, none indigenous, mostly researchers. I needed to take a writing trip for this book, and the theme seemed to fit the location. So with my wife and sons' permissions, I signed on to the icebreaker expedition ship *Ocean Nova* with seventy other passengers from a variety of countries. It was a fifteen-day trip: five to get there, five to explore, five to return home. Antarctica is difficult to reach.

Most of my time was spent researching and writing this book on the boat, taking breaks to sightsee. However, on the morning I am describing, I had taken a Zodiac dinghy from the *Ocean Nova* to the glacier for the skiing excursion. I was in a group of about fifteen other passengers and two guides. When we disembarked from the dinghy, we made a vertical climb to an open area where we then put on our skis and poles, divided into two teams, and started uphill in the snow. Within an hour or so we were at the crest, looking from the top in all directions. I have never in my life seen anything as strange and beautiful as that place. Mile after mile of intense, white, dazzling mountains and valley surrounded by a deep blue ocean and a lighter-colored sky, a blue so bright it was almost painful to look at. The cover of this book is a photograph I shot on the excursion. The small figures at the top are the other team, who reached the summit before our group did.

The wild beauty and scale of that place actually created a spiritual experience for me that I had not anticipated. It is difficult to describe, but I simply experienced a deep sense of closeness to God. I still feel it as I write these words. It was as if somehow I was face-to-face simultaneously with several aspects of His nature: His vastness, His power, His beauty, and His love, all moving toward me in waves. I felt very small but not at all alone. In a way I had not expected, I found God in worship. It was quite moving, an almost surreal experience.

The moment passed for me, and our team explored the area awhile longer. Our guides headed us back for the trip down to the dinghy. However, within a few minutes they noticed a problem: the shifting wind had unexpectedly created a hard sheet of ice over the path we had gone on in our ascent up the glacier. The ice made skiing extremely slippery and difficult. On top of that, our return path was on a downhill angle toward the ocean in two directions, both forward and to the left. In other words, we were, at one time, both pointed toward, and slanting toward, the sea below us. The guides immediately told us to stop moving and linked us to one another with ropes. Once we were secured, they set about hammering long stakes deep into the ice, one next to our lead person and one about one hundred feet ahead of that one. They fastened a rope between those stakes to serve as a makeshift fence. These stakes would be anchored enough that we could slowly move single file between them, holding onto the rope. Then we would stand still while our guides pulled up the back stake, took it to the front, and secured that one. Then we would repeat the procedure.

This was an extremely slow process, but it was the only way to get back in relative safety. We would be standing motionless, balancing on a sideways angle, sometimes for ten to fifteen minutes at a stretch. What made things worse was the isolation in which each member of our team found themselves. Though we were roped together, we were about ten feet apart. Facing the same direction, standing apart, and hearing the brush of the wind in our ears, we had no way to communicate. The only break we had was when a guide would tell us to start moving again, and we'd shuffle a few more feet toward the boat.

At first, the whole sequence of events was an adventure for me, a sort of danger-adrenaline rush. I thought, *What a killer story to tell back home!* However, after some time had passed and my legs began to tire, my mind shifted from adventure to something much more like fear. I began to wonder how many members of my team, to whom I was tethered, might have bad knees that would give way, which ones might become exhausted and fall down, who might suffer from a panic attack and fall, and who might even have a heart attack. I wondered, were they to start slipping and sliding down the hill, how many of them it would take to pull the rest of us into the ocean. I found myself thinking I might be in serious trouble. I started inventorying my life: Did my wife and sons know I love them, and would they be OK? Was I caught up in my relationships with my friends? Had I accomplished whatever mission I was supposed to? How long would I survive in a 33-degree ocean? Would this hurt a lot? Would God save me from this? Was I ready to meet Him? I confess I didn't think a great deal about my teammates' welfare, at least, not as much as I wish I had. At that point, it was pretty much all about me. Not having been through a lot of near-death experiences, I had no protocol or procedure in my mind to tell me how to do this correctly.

At any rate, it was during these hours that I experienced God in a different way, not the worshipful experience I had had earlier. I was in a bad state. I needed to know He was there when there was absolutely nothing I could do to change the situation around me. I needed to know what He was doing for me right then. I didn't know what was going on around me. And I needed to know that I was going to be OK. It was the "Where are you? I need help!" prayer. And though it is hard to describe, He answered. While I was thinking about my life and what was going to happen to me, in a few minutes I began to feel peace inside. I calmed down. My fear began to resolve. I experienced a sense that things would be OK. It wasn't that I was getting some sort of assurance that I would survive the day. Actually, I had no sense one way or another of the outcome. It was simply that He was with me, and I was going to be all right. Though very different than my experience a few hours before, this encounter with God was no less profound.

The step-by-step process to get us to the dinghy crawled along for several hours. Eventually, using this method, our guides, whose competence I believe saved our lives, returned us to the dinghy and, eventually, the boat. A fifteen-minute trek ended up taking us three hours. Finally safely aboard, we celebrated, and the trip resumed. But today I still carry with me these two "God experiences." They are unique. They remain useful to me today because they remind me of things I need to draw on in my life. I think of the first when I need to remember that He is full of power and grace, a Being with whom I want to connect. The second experience reminds me that when times are difficult and don't make sense, God is there.

# HARD TIMES MAKE US LOOK FOR GOD

I begin this book with the glacier narrative because it illustrates what most of us feel today during difficult times and circumstances. Whatever our situation, we feel some sense of confusion, anxiety, and helplessness. At the same time, we think about God and wonder where He is. The fact that you are reading this book indicates these two likelihoods about you. You, as well as others you care about, are struggling in some area of life. You are also concerned about what God's role is during these difficulties. We are living in hard times these days, all of us in our country and all over our world. And an incredible number of people, every day, are asking, "Where is God?" They want to know what He is doing in these times, how He can make a difference, and what they can do in that process.

Today, hard times come to us in several ways:

- FUNCTIONAL PROBLEMS. These struggles have to do with the task or "doing" areas of life, such as money or job issues. The global economic downturn that is happening as this book is being written is an example, with multitudes of us suffering severe financial or employment losses. In the areas of work and finances, life is breaking down for many. You or people you know well lose a home, a career, or retirement in a terrible flurry of events. People are confused, concerned, and afraid for their futures.
- HEALTH ISSUES. Medical and health problems come in all shapes and sizes. Diseases, such as cancer and heart problems, and accident-related issues, such as limb paralysis, are striking you or those you care about.
- CATASTROPHES. Natural disasters, such as tsunamis, hurricanes, and pandemics, ravage entire populations. Man-made horrors,

such as corrupt governments and genocides, cause unimaginable suffering, the kind for which there are no words.

- RELATIONAL CONFLICTS AND LOSSES. Sometimes things go seriously wrong in your relationships with people close to you. A marriage struggles or ends. An important dating relationship is damaged. Family members are alienated. Children get into serious trouble with drugs or develop acting-out issues. You lose a friendship. Someone you care about dies an untimely death. Since relationships are what life is about, it is very difficult to deal with these hardships.
- EMOTIONAL STRUGGLES. Often created or made worse by some combination of the above problems, people experience depression, anxiety issues, and addictions. These hardships are debilitating and no less difficult to bear than anything else.

The list could go on and on. There is almost no limit to the struggles that we experience in life. People are being affected in moderate and major ways. They often feel overwhelmed and can't think past the next day. "Normal" answers don't work. Life is not as predictable as it seemed yesterday. As stresses increase, the focus on the bad times increases. And most of the time, these difficulties are beyond their abilities to resolve. If they could have fixed it by now, they probably would have. Hard times are often the headlines in the news, the topic of conversation at work, at home, and in friendships. People are asking each other what they know that might help. They are asking themselves what resources they possess to solve the crises. And they are looking to God for hope and help.

There is a word in the Bible that describes this condition well. It is *affliction*. It is used to depict the suffering of the ancient Israelites under the slavery and oppression of Egypt (Ex. 1:11–12). Their slave masters afflicted them over and over again for years in a miserable existence. The word *afflicted* in the Hebrew language, as used in this passage, means "to become low." It conveys the sense of a downward direction of life, not an upward direction. That is an accurate description of so many people's experiences today. We are, as a people, carrying huge burdens: financial, medical, relational, and emotional. And the impossible weight of these burdens brings our countenances, attitudes, and focus downward, as if our backs are being bent over underneath the mass. People's afflictions are their many hard times.

As a psychologist, I see people in my office who are deeply affected by their life circumstances. As I mentioned above, hard times heavily influence our emotional and psychological conditions. A healthy, normal person who experiences personal trauma or abuse, for example, will sometimes develop depression or an anxiety disorder. The disorder is the symptom of the psychological injury. However, in addition to that symptom, an individual who already suffers from an emotional struggle will often experience a worsening of the symptom when he encounters difficult circumstances. For example, a financial crisis, job stress, relationship issue, or health scare can increase the severity of the disorder, making depression, addiction, or anxiety worse. The added pressure, stress, and drain of the circumstance create more of an issue and require more help and treatment to resolve it. In other words, *an external crisis often worsens the internal state.*

Sometimes the scale of suffering has an extremely wide range, from up close and personal (such as a friend facing a terminal illness) to an international level, on a much larger scale almost impossible to really understand. I have spoken at national conferences in places such as Africa, Sri Lanka, and India that have such unbelievable levels of need and suffering that I have to concentrate on staying emotionally present instead of just clicking off my brain. I have great respect for the pastors, leaders, missionaries, and relief workers in those regions, for their ability to stay "in the moment" and keep perspective in the face of large-scale suffering.

But whatever kind of suffering we face, we humans can't solve our problems alone. And when we encounter struggles larger than our abilities to fix them, God comes to mind more often, more seriously, and more intensely. We look to the sky and ask, "Where are You? What are You doing in this situation? When will You step in?" We want and need answers and guidance. These questions are the right ones to ask. They are not a blame game or a lack of faith, as some people think. They are actually part of the way that God designed us. Hard times cause us to stop what we are doing and seek Him.

## WIRED TO LOOK FOR GOD

It is not the entire truth to say that we look for God only during hard times. There is another reality: God has also designed us to seek Him in the first place. All through the Bible and human history, people have sought out God: "Seek the LORD and His strength; Seek His face evermore!" (1 Chron. 16:11 NKJV); "I seek your precepts" (Ps. 119:45 NASB). Sometimes this seeking comes from the perspective of a child's curiosity: is God beyond the solar system? Sometimes it is philosophical: does He exist, and if so, what is He like? And sometimes it is a search for meaning, purpose, and a connection with Him. The bottom line is this: we are beings who search for God in some fashion. We tend to want to go it alone, walk our own paths: "There is none who understands; There is none who seeks after God" (Rom. 3:11 NKJV). But we still think of Him and His ways.

There also may be a neurobiological aspect to the where-is-God question. Current research using brain-scan technology is finding that several areas of the brain become activated or "light up" when people pray, reflect on religious statements, or recall significant personal experiences with God. While there seems to be no specific "God spot" in the brain, there are findings that indicate some sort of a "God neural network" exists. This research does not prove or disprove God's existence. However, the point is that we do react in neurologically predictable ways when seeking God. He—and what He does with us—is extremely important to us.[1]

## THE ABSTRACTION AND THE REAL

The term *difficult times* doesn't mean a lot to us when we aren't experiencing them. We are concerned when we read about mass killings in Africa or a widespread disease in Asia, but we see those every day in the news, and it is easy to become anesthetized to them. These types of difficult times are an abstraction, something we think about and possibly even try to find some way we can help.

But hard times become more of a reality when they hit people we are close to. A neighbor has to move because of a home foreclosure. A relative gets a pink slip. A good friend gets bad news from the doctor. That is less abstract. We worry more and use more energy trying to help.

The final level of reality is when hard times happen to us. We are the one with the bad medical news or the job loss or the impending divorce or a depression we can't kick. Now it's really real.

I make this point because that is most likely why you are reading this book. Something bad has happened to you, either recently or a long time ago. And whatever it is, it was something that hurt you in a significant way, in a significant area of your life. Not only that, but your efforts to undo it have not worked.

That is important because this book is not really about solving our philosophical questions about the presence of God in hard times, though that is a part of it. It is more about helping you, as a real person in a real situation, find the hope and help that God provides.

In reality, hard circumstances are not the exception in human history but the norm. It is normal to think that life should play according to certain rules, and it often does. However, people have struggled at many levels through the centuries. And they have struggled with God and found answers in Him throughout those centuries. This is the human condition. So don't shy away from being aware of your situation. Remember that God is with His people. Our hope is in Him, as you'll discover as you read this book.

## THE ORGANIZING PRINCIPLES

There are three organizing principles that will help you to apply this material in the difficult situation you may find yourself. They will serve as anchors to help you understand and implement the ideas here. They are the themes running through this book.

### I. GOD IS FOR YOU.

Though your experience may indicate that God has forgotten you or has left you alone, He is on your side. He is the God of grace, and He is actively working on your behalf. The essence of grace is that God is for you. Grace is God's undeserved favor. That is, He wants to help us in hard times and ultimately to help us become the person He intended us to be. When Paul the apostle asked for help with his own thorn in the flesh, God's answer was grace: "My grace is sufficient for you, for My strength is made perfect in weakness" (2 Cor. 12:9 NKJV). So this book will present different aspects of how God gives us grace in our struggles. His grace may come in a way you don't expect or even in a way you wouldn't have wanted in the first place. But God is for you nonetheless.

A friend of mine was recently telling me about her own faith journey. She is a professional woman in the education sector. She is also raising three kids with her husband, and one of them is a special-needs child. Her life has not been easy; it has involved a tremendous amount of caring for others, often to the point that she feels drained. She told me that recently she had to go in for a biopsy. She was understandably afraid and concerned. But something happened right before the biopsy, something that had never happened to her in her life. She said, "I was thinking about the biopsy, and all of a sudden I experienced Jesus cradling me. He had His arms around me and told me it was going to be OK. I have never had that happen before. But after that, I wasn't afraid anymore." My friend is a very grounded and mature woman, not prone to wishful or delusional thinking. God showed my friend He was for her during her time of need. And that was all she needed for that trial.

The idea that "God is for you" is one of the guiding lights in my life and work. When you are struggling and see no evidence of God, it is easy to forget that He cares for us. But it is true. And it is no feel-good slogan either. It is one of the fundamental truths of the universe that we need to continually remind ourselves of, and it helps us through the valleys.

## 2. YOUR EXPERIENCE MATTERS.

Though this book's purpose is to help you make sense of and find answers for your struggles, at the same time it is very important to pay attention to what you are going through these days and how you feel about your situation. You may be experiencing a great deal of stress, hurt, or suffering, perhaps even at unimaginable levels. You may have anxiety, fear, confusion, anger, sadness, and a host of other negative emotions. You may simply be living day to day, hour to hour. That is just the reality of life today.

If you are in that position now, you need to be heard, understood, and supported, just as much as you need clarity of mind and understanding.

The last thing you need is to feel that your pain or anxiety should not be there or that it is dismissed, disregarded, or negated. That would not help you at all. So remember that *your experience, especially the negative part, matters to God and to those who care about you.* The answers found in this book aren't about forgetting all that and putting on a happy face. Nor are they about simply looking at bad things in a good light. My goal is for you to see your situation in the light of reality and to find hope in what God is doing for you.

It is easy to think that we should put up a brave front and stay positive about all our struggles. But that is not the biblical model. David, the man after God's own heart, got right to it and spilled out his guts about his own experience:

> How long, O LORD? Will You forget me forever?
>> How long will You hide Your face from me?
> How long shall I take counsel in my soul,
>> Having sorrow in my heart daily?
>> How long will my enemy be exalted over me?
> —Psalm 13:1–2 (NKJV)

To God, your experience matters. So it should matter to you as well. It will help you to move ahead on your journey toward healing if you focus on your experience and what it means rather than enter into comparisons. Comparisons can distort reality. Even more, they get you focused on what is not helpful and distract you from what is helpful. Comparisons can minimize how severe your situation is, such as thinking, *Lots of people in other countries have it much worse than I do, so I should stop feeling bad.* That sort of guilt message isn't really helpful. Your situation is yours, and your pain is yours. No one should judge your level of pain by what kind of life you have. A successful business person who loses a career that he loves and has been dedicated to for decades is truly suffering. He may have a home and a car, but he can be in great distress. He needs help in his situation, just as he is.

### 3. THE BIBLE IS OUR SOURCE FOR UNDERSTANDING GOD'S WAYS IN HARD TIMES.

A great deal of the Bible's teachings and narratives have to do with this subject. In fact, the central message of the Bible is about God redeeming a humanity that is in trouble and suffering. The Scriptures don't answer every one of our issues and queries about human difficulty, at least, not in ways that we would expect. As we will see, they leave room for mystery, and they also require faith. But there are helpful models, insights, comforts, challenges, and steps the Bible gives us, which can help us in our paths. In my personal life and in my study, I have spent a great deal of time in the Psalms, the book of Job, and the four Gospels to help me figure out what makes sense. You can trust God's Word in the same way that you can trust God himself: "The entirety of Your word is truth, / And every one of Your righteous judgments endures forever" (Ps. 119:160 NKJV).

# CHAPTER 1

# POWER, PRESENCE, AND PROTEST

I n researching this book over the past several months, I have asked a good number of people what the phrase *Where is God?* actually means to them and if it resonates for them at some level. I have yet to hear one neutral answer, such as, "I don't know. It sounds boring, irrelevant—no interest." If fact, the answers have been quite the opposite. People have said:

- "It's something I think about a lot these days."
- "Oh my gosh, I ask the question whenever I look at the news."
- "I thought that when I got sick."
- "Yes, where was God when I was laid off?"
- "I have friends in hard times whom I have no answer for."
- "Didn't Larry King ask that on his show the other night?"

However universal the phrase may be, the idea has several understandings for different people and for different situations. We don't all mean the same thing when we ask, "Where is God?" I have found there are three different questions people ask when they think or say it.

## THE POWER QUESTION

I was at a restaurant the other night, and a three-year-old boy was walking around the tables nearby his family. He came to a stop directly behind a waiter who was taking an order, at an angle from which the waiter couldn't see him. When the waiter turned around, he tripped over the child. Luckily, he was very agile and broke his fall at the last second and avoided landing on the boy. Nevertheless, it was a loud and abrupt event, the kind where people around stopped talking to see what had happened. I jumped out of my chair to help, but things were OK.

From the little boy's point of view, however, things were not OK. Immediately, he made a beeline for his dad's chair and crawled into his lap, crying. This response was not one he had to think about. He automatically looked for his parent during a stressful situation that was beyond his ability to fix or understand. He headed for someone who had the power to make things all right again.

As adults, we have the same need for God when we are in tough times. A situation is over our heads, beyond our capacity to fix, and is not getting better. We ask, "Where is God?", and it is a question of His power, His capacity, and His ability to fix a bad situation. We don't have the resources or wisdom to handle the problem ourselves. We need a miracle. We want His power to restore our health, find a good job, or put together a fractured relationship. We look to God for the answer, and that is the right direction to look.

Our tendency is to be strong, self-sufficient, and dependent on our own willpower, but rather than try harder, we should reach out to the God who is all-powerful: "Ah, Lord GOD! Behold, You have made the heavens and the earth by Your great power and outstretched arm. There is nothing too hard for You" (Jer. 32:17 NKJV). This is the question I was asking on the Antarctic glacier. When I was in trouble and contemplating falling into the freezing ocean, I wanted power. Protection. Action. A miracle. The strong hand and powerful arm of God.

I have also noticed during this economic downturn that more of my friends talk about God in this way. That is, friends who aren't involved in church or spiritual activities are looking for God. I was at a party with a neighbor who had been laid off, and he mentioned prayer to me, a subject he and I had never broached. The context was that he was praying for a job opportunity. As a result, our conversation took a deeper and more meaningful turn than it ever had before.

So be aware that your question may be a real question, a search for One who can move mountains and do miracles, for He can.

## THE PRESENCE QUESTION

Sometimes these three words indicate a desire, some sort of longing for a relationship of closeness and intimacy with God. It is what a wife says to her husband at dinner, when he seems preoccupied or distant: "Where are you?" Meaning, "I can't experience your presence or your heart right now. The lights are on, but nobody's home. What's going on inside you?" She feels a little lost or disoriented, not knowing what he is feeling inside. She is asking for presence, for "being there."

We are designed for more than simply receiving power from God, a relationship in which He does superhero feats to help us. Ultimately, we long for His presence, a connection of closeness with God: "As the deer pants for the water brooks, / So pants my soul for You, O God" (Ps. 42:1 NKJV). God's love for us goes far beyond rescuing us.

He wants to be with us in a deep and abiding way. He seeks us out. In fact, before we ever asked, "Where is God?" He first asked the same question of us: "Then the Lord God called to Adam and said to him, 'Where are you?'" (Gen. 3:9 NKJV). He is the real seeker, not us.

It's hard to ask the presence question during difficult times. Struggle and pain come to the forefront and take up our energy and attention. We don't tend to be all that relationally oriented in the middle of a crisis. My presence experience with God happened at the glacier's summit, when things were perfectly beautiful. I would have had to make an effort not to appreciate God then; His presence was all encompassing at that moment. Presence, however, gave way to a need for power when the winds and ice hit us.

Yet one of the signs that we are growing in faith is when we begin to seek God's presence when things are dark and hard. Continuing to seek Him when He doesn't come up with the power goods, as we would like Him to do, but recognizing He is there still, comforting and encouraging us, indicates a deepening and maturing of our inner selves as we continue to let him develop us.

Today, I showed my sons, Ricky and Benny, the passage Job 13:15 in the Bible: "Though He slay me, yet will I trust Him" (NKJV). It is one of the most difficult and profound statements of faith in the Bible. We talked about the reality that, while we are to ask for God's power to help solve our problems, the spiritual life doesn't stop there. Ultimately, if He takes everything away, if He doesn't relieve the problems, and if He even takes us down, too, we are to seek Him and hope in Him. I didn't want to discourage the boys from hoping for a good life—I hope they have great lives. But I wanted them to also see that there is something beyond our circumstances, and that is an emotional, from-the-heart connection to God, no matter what is going on in our lives. We will explore this more fully in the chapter on hard times and faith.

# THE QUESTION THAT IS NOT A QUESTION

Finally, sometimes "Where is God?" is not actually a question. In my work as a psychologist, I have found this to be a significant issue. For many people who struggle, there is no real and true answer to the where-is-God question that will satisfy them. No explanation from a theological level, a spiritual level, a psychological level, or any level will make a difference to their current conditions. That is because many times, "Where is God?" is not actually a question they're willing to receive an answer to. It is a protest. It is a statement of how badly they hate what is going on. It is a desire, a wish, a cry of pain and anguish. It is an emotional reaction to a great difficulty. The desire simply says, *I want things to be better.* I want the bad times to go away so I can live my normal life. I want my child to straighten out. I want my husband to love me. I want to feel better, not sicker. I want to find a mate. I want a job so I can take care of my family. I simply hate what is going on, and I want things to be different. These are protests, not questions.

The most profound and moving where-is-God question that has ever been asked in history is that of Jesus in His own agony on the cross: "My God, My God, why have You forsaken Me?" (Matt. 27:46 NKJV). He was not asking for clarification, an answer, or an explanation. He knew what was going on behind His pain. He knew every reason for what He was experiencing, for He had planned and predicted His own suffering. Speaking to His disciples, He said, "Listen . . . we're going up to Jerusalem, where the Son of Man will be betrayed to the leading priests and the teachers of religious law. They will sentence him to die. Then they will hand him over to the Romans to be mocked, flogged with a whip, and crucified. But on the third day he will be raised from the dead" (Matt. 20:18–19 NLT). In that moment of pain, Jesus was uttering the question that was not a question.

We often see this in parenting. Kids will ask why they can't watch

TV all night or eat junk food or text message during dinner. And as every good parent knows, you answer the question once or twice, and then you say, "I've given you all the reasons I have. Maybe this is more about you just wanting me to change the rule. I'm sorry, but the rule stands."

Our teenage kids still don't like our curfew rules. But my wife and I finally figured out that after we explained our position several times, they were no longer asking us a real question. It was a desire couched in a question: "I want you to let me stay out later." That helps. When we realized this, we no longer wasted time reasoning when reason isn't the issue at all. So it is helpful when we struggle to think about what we mean deep inside when we ask, "Where is God?" Am I trying to make sense of something that seems insane or evil? Or am I in such distress that I simply have a very strong desire for things to change, and it comes out of my mouth as a question? If it's a true question, then we can be open to the possibility of answers. If it's a desire, our efforts need to go toward either doing what we can to achieve that desire or toward learning how to grieve, let something go, adapt to the painful reality, and move on. So the nature of "Where is God?" will direct you to what your next steps are to be.

I have also found that this question can be about protest and understanding at the same time. On the radio program I cohost, *New Life Live!*, a caller will often ask about a spouse's behavior and emotional distance. A wife will say, "I want to know why my husband won't talk to me on a deeper level." I'll ask her some questions and get background information on the relationship. At some point I may offer an explanation like, "It may be that he experiences intimacy as unsafe, and he may believe, if he opens up, he'll be rejected or put down," or something to that effect. In all the thousands of calls I have ever heard on the program, I do not remember one in which the caller then said, "OK. I just wanted to know why he's like that. Thanks, bye." Not once.

The call always evolved to, "How can he open up more?" or "What can I do to help him?" or "What is the next step?" We can also be that way with God. "Where are you?" can be both a protest against a problem and a search for understanding and perspective.

# CHAPTER 2

# WHY ASK WHY?

M y wife, Barbi, and I are both kid-loving people by nature. Her entire career has been in the public elementary school system, and I was raised in a large family. We have loved having our two sons. However, during our childbearing years, Barbi had two miscarriages. Our sadness and disappointment in those periods were profound. We were aware that statistically, half of all pregnancies end that way and that these are very common losses for couples. Still, we grieved, and it took some time for the feelings to resolve. We felt the emptiness of where we thought those children should be, in our home and in our lives.

Like most parents who go through this, I spent time asking God why we encountered these losses. I don't remember thinking that God had treated me unfairly or unjustly. Many of my friends and the people I have counseled have felt that way, so I understand it, but I didn't feel it. In my case, it was more that I wanted to make sense of the loss if I could. The issue was, *I'd like to know why this happened.* And it was certainly a lingering question in my grief.

Fortunately, we had some very caring and supportive friends who helped a great deal. They spent time with us during those days. They were warm and they were present, and that is what made the most difference. The most helpful ones simply asked how we were doing and listened to us talk, sometimes praying with us. They made themselves available to us.

At the same time, other friends were a little less helpful, though not intentionally so. Their approaches didn't help us really move on from our loss. One lady, for example, who had her own struggle with God, talked to us about how unfair it is that there are so many loving parents who can't have more kids. Another said that God had a special reason for this, and it would become clear to us. And another told us it was simply nature's way of solving a problem. Though I appreciated the sentiments, these ideas didn't move me down the path of resolving my sadness. They seemed to make things worse instead of better.

In time, however, the emotions dissipated for us, through our friends, God, time, and the grief process. It has been several years since those days. I don't think about the miscarriages often anymore, though the feelings of sadness about the loss of a potential wonderful relationship still do arise occasionally. In fact, when I was talking to Barbi about these losses in preparation for writing this book, our sad feelings returned to us. But that is what memory is about. It's a way of honoring someone who matters to us. I would never want to forget these kids, even though I never knew them. I have returned to today's path, relationships, and responsibilities, and that is where I live. I don't know what God's specific purpose was in those times of loss. But I don't really feel that I need to. However, over the years, in my own studies and experience, I have found some ideas which have made sense for me and which are the subject of this chapter.

When we are in tough circumstances, most people ask a second question in addition to, "Where is God?" It is, "Why does God allow suffering?" In other words, how can a loving, caring divinity allow us to be in crisis, have sicknesses, and encounter natural disasters? Is He unloving or powerless or judging us or what? This is one of the most often-asked questions in human history. There have been innumerable books written on the subject. I recently searched the phrase *God and suffering* on Amazon.com, and the result was over seventeen thousand books. This is an important and significant question. We all need to grapple with it, and hopefully we'll come to some sort of conclusion that makes sense.

The two questions are related. The *why* is more theological and philosophical in nature and is concerned about understanding the concepts and abstracts. The *where* is somewhat more personal and has more to do with an interest in God's ways, His activities, and how we can interact with Him in times of difficulty. As a psychologist, I have found that when people are experiencing struggles, such as the ones we are dealing with, they often want to talk about the more conceptual issues before they get into the emotions, the process of healing, and the action steps they need. This can be very helpful. By doing this, they are not avoiding pain or discomfort or retreating into an imaginary world of ideas. They are, in fact, working on creating a foundation or a thinking paradigm for themselves so they can better understand what is going on. It is similar to a person who finds he needs surgery and asks his physician every possible question about the procedure. The information helps him feel less anxious, less confused, and a little more in control of matters.

As I mentioned earlier, the question of why difficult times occur is a well-researched topic. It is thousands of years old and is one of the central issues in philosophy, theology, and psychology. Many intelligent, educated, thoughtful, and spiritual people have wrestled long and hard with this question. The ancient Greek philosopher Epicurus has the first recorded statement of the problem from an intellectual perspective:

Is God willing to prevent evil, but not able?
Then is he impotent.
Is he able, but not willing?
Then is he malevolent.
Is he both able and willing?
Whence then is evil?[1]

Centuries earlier, however, Job asked the same question from a much more personal and in-the-moment perspective: "Why is life given to those with no future, those God has surrounded with difficulties?" (3:23 NLT). The reality that this topic has been so thoroughly discussed means that you will benefit from knowing what others have said. The point here is to make sure you read some of the thoughtful books about the question of God and hard times. (You can find some suggestions in the appendix section of this book.) You will agree with some and disagree with others because they do not agree with each other. And if you are jarred by something abnormal going on in your life, if you are concerned about why bad things happen to good people, or if you want to make sense of the character of God in a world that doesn't work, I think you have a healthy curiosity about some very important things.

You have your own losses and your own unanswered questions about why you had to go through them. Your questions may be philosophical, such as why would God allow world hunger or war; or personal, such as why your marriage is struggling, why you have a health problem, or why you were laid off. But these are good questions that people should and do ask. When you try your best to be a decent person, treat others with respect, and take responsibility for your own problems, how do you make sense of some tragedy blasting in like a hurricane and creating a chaos that you had no part in? "Why does God allow hard times?" is a worthwhile question to consider.

WHY ASK WHY?

# WHY WE ASK WHY

It is helpful to understand where the *why* question comes from in the first place. There are two primary reasons we ask this question.

## 1. NORMAL DOESN'T HAPPEN.

When life doesn't play by the rules, it's understandable to pay attention to that. You are noticing that something isn't making sense. You are seeing some aberration from what we expect from life. Suppose, for example, you and your spouse get home after work. He is normally a pretty warm and stable guy. After years of marriage, you expect a kiss, a hug, and a few minutes of catching up before you go on to kids and dinner. But this day there is no kiss or hug. He paces around the room. He is distant and looks preoccupied. He tries to listen to your day, but he is obviously thinking about something else. What are you thinking at this time? You're thinking that something is wrong, and most likely you ask, "Are you OK? Is something wrong?" Hopefully you find out what is bothering him. You see something in a person whom you know very well, something that is out of the norm and doesn't make sense. So you question it. You don't say to yourself, *I'm sure things are OK, and it's going to be fine. I'll just act like things are normal.* At least I hope you wouldn't. We psychologists call that denial!

Many people have had the jarring experience of driving through an intersection on a green traffic light and being narrowly missed, or worse, by someone running the red light. Besides fright and terror, the sensation is also one of shock. Something that normally doesn't happen just happened. You expected the other driver to stop on red as most people do, and he didn't. Something was wrong.

Those experiences show that we carry within us an expectation for a normal life. That is, we anticipate that the events of the day will occur in some sort of predictable pattern, at least within a range of

13

what seems reasonable. We'll drive successfully to work. We'll have a productive day. We'll be with family or friends that night, and so forth. We see life as having an expectable outcome, within some parameters. This is built through your life experiences. Having the same basic patterns for years builds up that sense of "normal."

So when events occur outside the normal range of what we are used to, we notice it. We experience what psychologists call *cognitive dissonance*. Cognitive dissonance is the discomfort we feel when something we know or believe is met with new information that doesn't seem to fit. For example, suppose you are really disappointed with the woman you are dating. Time after time, she has let you down. Then, the day you are ready to break up, she tells you she loves you with all her heart. You go into a quandary. The new info doesn't match with the old.

In the same way, difficult times create cognitive dissonance. You expected to keep your job, but you were laid off. You expected to stay healthy, but you contracted a disease. You expected to have kids, but you faced infertility. So, you notice that things aren't going the way you expected and you ask, reasonably, "Why is this happening?"

That question easily leads to "Why is God allowing this bending of the normal rules?" I think it is normal to pay attention when things aren't normal. In fact, I think it is strange when people tell me they have never had these sorts of questions. Not many people will actually say that, but some will. They will say, "I know God is taking care of me, so none of this bothers me at all," or "It's all going to be good," or "Just trust and think positive." I agree that, in time, those may be good perspectives to have. But *in that very moment* and at that very instant in time, if a person never questions an unusual or bad event, something is wrong.

In addition, some people have a distorted idea of what normal is. Their life experiences involved hurtful or chaotic events and relationships, so they don't have a healthy or safe idea of normal. For them, normal could mean, "people can't be trusted," or "you're on your own in life with no help," or "the good times will be ruined by the bad times." People who grow up with an alcoholic parent, for example, will often say they have no idea of what a normal family life is because they never saw it. Individuals who have had these sorts of experiences will sometimes not be as bothered by difficult times as those who had more predictably safe environments. They will sometimes say, "When I became ill, I sort of expected it; that's the pattern in my life." That is not a healthy sign, obviously, but a sign of injury causing a distortion in their perception of the world.

## 2. GOD CALLS HIMSELF LOVING AND JUST IN A BROKEN WORLD.

The second reason we ask the question, "Why?" has to do with God Himself and how He describes Himself to be. It involves claims He makes and holds Himself to. It revolves around His nature and character. The Bible says that love and justice are part of who He is:

"He loves whatever is just and good; the unfailing love of the LORD fills the earth" (Ps. 33:5 NLT).

"Unfailing love and truth have met together. Righteousness and peace have kissed!" (Ps. 85:10 NLT).

"So the Word became human and made his home among us. He was full of unfailing love and faithfulness" (John 1:14 NLT).

Over and over, God identifies Himself with these two qualities. He says that He cares. And He says that He is just. The first quality has to do with His heart and His concern for us. The second has to do with His standards and sense of right and wrong. So this naturally leads to the question that if God cares, and if God believes in justice, how do you make sense of His care for a world that does not operate according to justice? This is different from a sense of *normal* and from a sense of *ideal*. It has more to do with a seeming disconnect in the very nature of God. And that is a great issue for many people.

I don't know how many times I have been with a friend or a client in a time of loss who will look at me in his pain and say, "Why did God let this happen to me?" No matter how many times I hear it, it is never an easy valley to walk through. And obviously, most of the time, that moment is not the right time to answer the question. What that person generally needs in that setting is to have room to protest and a person to be with him. But later, in a more stable setting, it is a question that deserves an answer.

The technical name for this problem is *theodicy*. The word refers to the study of understanding God's goodness in the face of evil. As I mentioned, it has been exhaustively researched and considered for thousands of years. It is a question that affects people deeply. And in the next two chapters, I present my own understanding of the answer to why God allows suffering. My point in all this is that the Bible's teachings on God's character and the existence of suffering are difficult to understand and are worth more than a superficial answer. (I have provided a brief appendix with overviews of some of the major works on the subject, if you want to go deeper into the topic.) Again, there are enough contrasting viewpoints on the why question that you could spend the rest of your life studying what has been written. But *why*? must be asked. At the same time, I hope you can land on the explanation that helps you understand God and the world. And most of all, I hope your explanation keeps you moving toward God in hope and love, not away from Him in disappointment.

# CHAPTER 3

# THE PIE CHART

God did not design life to be as difficult as it is. His original plan did not include your current hard circumstances. We were not meant to experience layoffs, loneliness, alienation, divorce, depression, or cancer. It was never part of the plan. Instead, life was supposed to have been a great, overwhelmingly positive experience. We were to have a continual, uninterrupted connection with God, intimate and safe relationships with each other, and a purposeful role and task in life. At the beginning of the creation of humanity, this was the picture: "So God created human beings in his own image. / In the image of God he created them; / male and female he created them. Then God blessed them and said, 'Be fruitful and multiply. Fill the earth and govern it.'" (Gen. 1:27, 28 NLT). God, one another, and a meaningful career—that is a fulfilling picture. When we look at the history of the human race, it is hard to imagine that things were as great as they were in the Garden, but that is the reality. It didn't used to be this way.

The best and simplest explanation for why life has become as difficult as it is today is embodied in the word *sin*. Now there is an emotionally charged word! *Sin* is a very unpopular term in today's culture, both religious and secular. For many people, the word *sin* evokes images of crazy, screaming, extremist preachers, or condemning and judgmental religious groups, or an intolerant and mean-spirited God. Who would want to use a word with that sort of baggage? In fact, psychologists are often trained to avoid the word so people won't feel guilty or judged. However, those images aren't true to the meaning of the word *sin*. It's a much-maligned term. The reality is that *sin* is actually a very helpful and useful word. I don't know if it will ever become popular in our culture again, but it explains a great deal about the way our world turns.

One of the clearest definitions of *sin* is "to miss the mark." That is simple and accurate. It is going off the desired path. We can all relate to that. Whatever the goal, when you don't hit the mark, that is sin. This applies at all levels of life. For example, it is a good thing to care for each other. So murder misses that mark and is a sin. Stealing someone's iPod misses the mark of being respectful of each other, so it is sin. So is fantasizing about someone else's spouse. In fact, when you think about it, we miss the mark in many ways all day: being late to an appointment, not performing our best at work, not taking the dog for a walk, ordering a burger when we should have had a salad, missing a tennis serve, or nicking our faces when shaving. There is no sting of condemnation in the word, though some sins are certainly more malevolent than others, and some are more intentional than others (Lev. 4:2–3). It is simply that we don't do the right thing, whatever that right thing is.

The inevitability that we will miss the mark is the core reason the universe is in the condition it is in. Like a virus at pandemic level, sin has spread through the world and infected all parts of it. It is so pervasive to us that it is the central reason that God the Father sent Jesus the Son to die: "For Christ also died for sins once for all, the just for the unjust . . ." (1 Pet. 3:18 NASB). And even though Jesus died for sin, this is an offer made by God that can be, and is often, refused. Because of this lack of response to God's grace, much of the world still suffers from the sin problem and has for thousands of years. More than that, the sin virus has mutated to three different categories, and when you understand these categories, it may help to see clearly what a difference sin has made in explaining our present difficulties.

## Sin by Us

This refers to those things we do that go against God's designated path for us. It is a universal reality about us, the human race: we all have a tendency to miss the mark. We may certainly have many strengths and positive qualities, but those don't negate the darker reality of the sin virus. Sometimes we sin because it's easier, or we're in a rush, or we don't want to listen to reason, or we care more about ourselves than others, for example. But we all come by "sin by us" honestly. David says it this way: "For I know my transgressions, and my sin is always before me" (Ps. 51:3 NIV). Our sin is a reality of our lives. If we are honest, we realize that it's something we do all the time.

On my Antarctic trip, we took an excursion to a small island that was populated by around a quarter million penguins, an incredible sight: tuxedos for miles and miles. Our guides took us down trails to watch them and take pictures. At one point, one of the guides spoke abruptly to us, telling us not to move. We looked around to see what was going on. A group of about twenty penguins was crossing the trail a few yards in front of us. We had figured we had the right of way, so to speak, as we were on the trail and the penguins were crossing it. But the guide explained, "We are in an ecosystem here. Anything we do other than observe can affect this system. If you make them go another direction, you are causing changes that have nothing to do with nature and their environment." In other words, we were in danger of *sinning* against the penguins and the ecosystem—that is, going against what was best by creating changes that could harm them.

The difficulties you are experiencing today, the ones that have motivated you to read this book, may have originated from outside yourself and may not have been your fault. If you suffered mistreatment in your home as a child, if you were hit by a car as you biked down the road, or if you had a healthy lifestyle but still got cancer, those things came from a source outside of your sin. Other difficulties, however, arise out of our sins. If as an adult you fed a tendency toward destructive sexual behaviors, if you were weaving in and out of the bike lane, or if you never worked out and ate too many fatty foods, you may have made a contribution to your condition.

This isn't any sort of blame game. I simply think one of the healthiest things anyone who is having problems can do is to ask, "How am I contributing to this?" In other words, we take the logs out of our eyes (Matt. 7:5). This could be an opportunity for you. If some of your experiences are caused by your own actions, then you may have some control or some choices over the outcomes. For example, when people become aware that their lifestyle contributes to a health problem, it's a wake-up call for them. They start working out and eating better. They are able to reverse some of their difficult circumstances because they pay attention to the "sin by them."

## Sin Against Us

Unfortunately, there are times when we suffer at the hands of another. These are situations in which there was no missing the mark on our part. But we are affected by someone else's sin against us, sometimes with devastating effect. For example:

- Your spouse lies to you.
- Your friend is harsh and condemning.

- Your parent is unavailable to meet your needs.
- Your spouse becomes abusive.
- Someone you trust is unfaithful.
- Your company is unethical in their financial dealings, causing you to suffer financial loss.
- Someone acts with physical violence toward you.

When we are sinned against, we are sometimes in a state of shock, especially if we are hurt by someone we trust and love. We don't anticipate someone we care about injuring us physically or emotionally. I remember when our son Ricky was about eight, he became obstinate about whether or not he should take out the trash. We went round and round about this, and I could get nowhere with him. I would try to reason with him, and he would have none of it. His agenda was not to take out the trash, no matter what. Finally, in frustration, I raised my voice at him. Immediately his face changed, and I could see fear in his eyes, which broke my heart. I stopped what I was saying and asked, "Am I scaring you?"

He said, "Yes, Dad, stop it. I don't like it!"

I was really broken, imagining what it was like for an eight-year-old to be in the presence of someone much larger, a person who was supposed to protect him but instead was so angry with him. I sat him down and said, "I am so very sorry. That was a bad thing for me to do. I know that really scared you, and I should never have done that." It took a few minutes of talking and listening to him, but he began to feel safer. We moved on from there. But my point is, I missed the mark, and Ricky experienced the effects. He was sinned against by me. And though I nipped it in the bud and focused on repairing the damage as soon as I realized what I was doing, it was still a hurtful thing to him.

We are sinned against both intentionally and unintentionally. Sometimes people hurt us because they want to hurt us or because they are angry and want to punish us. Sometimes they are simply self-absorbed or out of touch and not aware of how deeply their actions affect us. Either way, it contributes to the suffering we experience. When I do a diagnostic session for depression, I ask about significant losses and hurtful relationships. A great many types of depressions have to do with being hurt in a significant relationship. And it probably goes without saying that all of us are both sinner and sinned against. We are each part of the muddled mix of the human race.

I was speaking to a spiritual growth ministry group recently, and we had an open-mike question-and-answer period after the talk. A man stood up and said, "I just need some advice about personal growth. I have had some bad stuff happen in the past few years. My wife left me for another man, and on top of that, she has been lying about me to get more custody of the kids. On top of that, I lost my job at around the same time, and I am running out of money for myself and for my support for them."

My heart went out to him, and I said, "If everything you are telling me is true, you don't have a character issue. You are in despair and need help." I was thinking about how sometimes being hurt has nothing to do with a personal area of weakness that is unearthed. As I saw in the case of this man, sometimes we are just broken and sinned against.

The man came up to me after the talk in tears. He said, "You have no idea how much I needed to hear that. I thought it was all because of some broken thing in me. But when you said it wasn't a character problem and that I needed help, I felt like someone understood." Sometimes, it is just about getting help and healing from despair. Make sure you understand the difference.

## SIN FROM A BROKEN WORLD SYSTEM

Sometimes bad things happen, but there is no bad guy to blame. The world simply doesn't work right. No one missed the mark, but the way things should have happened didn't happen. The world missed the mark. It is like those times when your computer freezes up and there is no apparent reason for it. The tech support guy scratches his head and says, "Sometimes computers just do things." He is right. Something just breaks. As the saying goes, "That's just the way it is."

Actually, it's not that simple. There is a reason for "the way it is." The world, creation, all of nature suffered when humanity missed the mark. Through no fault of its own, the world is broken: "For the creation was subjected to futility, not willingly, but because of Him who subjected it, in hope that the creation itself also will be set free from its slavery to corruption into the freedom of the glory of the children of God" (Rom. 8:20–21 NASB). In other words, there was a trickle-down effect. The world has endured some contamination from our sin, which makes sense. How can humanity have dominion over the world and not break things? And creation won't be free of sin's stronghold until the time God steps in and changes things. Here are some examples of the broken system we experience:

- Natural disasters, such as tsunamis and earthquakes
- Illness of a loved one
- A job loss due to a company's losing market share to its competition
- The effects of growing up with a mentally ill parent
- The birth of a child with some physical challenge
- The untimely death of someone we love deeply

The broken-world-system aspect of sin lends itself to the where-is-God question because we struggle to understand our situation when bad things happen but there is no villain, no one to blame. You can sometimes live with the reality that people let us down, for we do the same to others. But when an infant dies of SIDS, or a hurricane kills an innocent family, or a disease wipes out a population, it simply goes beyond the pale of any easy answer. These matters of natural catastrophes and broken-world problems are very difficult to understand and accept. Often, we simply don't know and will not know the why of these. Dr. J. P. Moreland, a Christian philosopher and author, says that it is a matter of our being unable to judge these events from the long-term perspective. From our human vantage point, we cannot know the ultimate long-term result of a catastrophe or loss. That perspective is not available to us; it is only available to God. So we can't judge its meaning or reason. This is not a statement with which anyone should comfort a person in grief, but it is a very helpful viewpoint from a more thoughtful and intellectual level.

## THE PERCENTAGES

When I am speaking on the topic of dealing with hard times, I often tell my audiences to think of any difficult situation they are presently in, and considering the three types of sin, attribute the causes of their particular problem. If you had a pie chart for your job problem, your emotional issue, or a relational struggle, you'd start with 100 percent. Then you'd figure what part is caused by you, what part you can attribute to someone else, and what part is caused by the world system we live in. Most of the time, it helps clarify why an issue is the way it is. For example, let's say you get laid off from your job. The problem may be 10 percent your doing, 30 percent others' fault, and 60 percent due to the world. Or your marriage is struggling, and you're considering divorce. This issue may be 40 percent your fault, 40 percent your spouse's, and 20 percent the world's. Certainly these are broad examples by necessity, but they are a good starting point.

How does a pie chart of the causes of your problems aid you beyond giving you an understanding of your situation? It is actually very helpful because the action steps of the three sin problems are all different in their nature. That is, the three sins have three very different solutions. For example, when the problem is us, the solution is to do what the Bible says: *repent*, which literally means "to change." We apologize, take responsibility, and reverse our ways. When others sin against us, we are to reconcile as much as possible, heal, guard ourselves from further injury, and forgive. When the world system acts against us, we are to be agents of justice in the world, involved in making the world a better place, and at the same time, we are to accept the way things are.

Using the example of my raising my voice with my son Ricky, I'd say that problem was perhaps 85 percent me, 5 percent him, and 10 percent the world. I was the grown-up and should have acted better. He was squirrely and obstinate, and that was his 5 percent contribution. And I had had a hard day at work with some business pressures, so 10 percent enters in there. Can you see how this doesn't justify me at all? (85 percent is a big number!) But it does help me: For the 85 percent, I had to repent, apologize, and change my ways. For the 5 percent, when he and I were OK, I later talked to him about his attitude about taking out the trash. That was the reconciliation part. And for the 10 percent, I accepted that my day at work was tough. It was nobody's fault, just a demanding day at work. So I worked on not taking work pressure home to my family. My point is, we aren't helpless when bad things happen. We can go beyond the question to why this is happening to us and come to an understanding. Then we can take some action.

## THE IDEAL AND THE REAL

The Bible paints a word picture of what that ideal world should look like: "In that day the wolf and the lamb will live together; the leopard will lie down with the baby goat. The calf and the yearling will be safe with the lion, and a little child will lead them all" (Isa. 11:6 NLT). It is a world of connectedness, safety, and peace. You could show that passage to just about anyone, and it would resonate inside them. It would reflect *the ideal world that already resides within that person.* That Bible verse didn't put that ideal there, God did. It is in each and every person's soul and heart. But we don't live in this ideal world—not yet.

The world we live in is fallen, and it gives us an idea of normal based on our experiences. Likewise, we have an idea of what is perfect, ideal, just, and fair, and that comes from a combination of God's design mixed with our experiences.

Not only do you carry the concept of an ideal world inside you, but you carry an ideal *you* inside as well. Reflect for a minute on how you perceive yourself. You have two images of you. One is the you that you are now, with various attributes, strengths, and weaknesses. You may be friendly, smart, caring, sometimes afraid or lazy, have great potential, and so on. That is the *real* you. The second you has to do with the person you would like to be one day, the one you are striving to be but aren't yet: more caring, successful, patient, and unafraid with your potential fully realized. That is the *ideal* you. It's good to have the ideal because it helps us stretch, grow, and become a better person.

The pie chart analysis can go a long way to help validate why you are asking, "Where is God?" Simply put, we ask it because the world isn't as it should be, and we know that truth deep inside. Life was not meant to be the way it is now. You are right for having that thought. In fact, God hardwired you to have that thought. Understanding the reasons for our actions will help us grow as we seek to understand God and this world more.

# CHAPTER 4

# FREEDOM IN THE SERVICE OF LOVE

W hy would a good God allow trouble and suffering? This is not simply a philosophical concern. It is important to your being able to trust, connect with, and follow God. If you have not been able to reconcile this, it is often difficult to feel safe with God and to reach out to him. It is foundational to approaching the entire where-is-God question.

A recent conversation illustrates the conclusion to this age-old question that I have personally reached. I was talking to Beth, an executive in a leadership coaching program I conduct in Southern California. In addition to her demanding work as vice president of a retail chain, she was also dealing with some struggles in her marriage. Beth's husband, Josh, had a tendency to disconnect emotionally and shut down. He would avoid deep conversations by either changing the subject or simply turning on the TV and shutting her out. It was extremely hurtful to her, and it disrupted the entire family. She often felt very alone and unsupported in her marriage.

I asked Beth what would be happening at the time her husband started to withdraw. I was thinking of all the possible reasons for his actions, such as a depression, an inordinate need for space, unresolved anger toward Beth, even an addiction. She said, "It tends to happen just at the time I need him most."

"Like what?"

"Like when I'm stressed-out from work, when the kids are going nuts, or when I just want him to talk because I need contact."

"OK, what happens when you bring this up?"

"I start talking about what's going on and ask him what he thinks, and he won't say anything."

"He'll just sit there and look at you?"

"Yes, pretty much. Then I'll say that he needs to listen to me and interact more, and he shuts down even more."

"Then what?"

"Well, then he may walk off to watch TV or get online."

"And then what do you do?"

"I get so upset that Josh isn't listening that I confront him and tell him to get off-line and look at me and talk to me."

"And then?"

"And then he may look at me some more, or he'll leave the room and walk outside or to the backyard."

"And you follow him."

"I have to. Nothing else will work. He needs to know that it isn't normal for a husband to be that out of it. I follow him and try to get him to connect."

I said, "I understand that he sounds deeply unresponsive to you. But I need for you to know that you will never get him to listen to you this way."

She didn't want to hear that. "But Josh isn't getting it, and I need him as a husband! I am not asking for anything unreasonable here." She began to get a little emotional as her loneliness emerged.

"I agree with you. But he isn't going to realize it that way. You are resisting and pushing against his freedom, and he will never move toward you and be a teammate as long as he feels that from you."

She said, "How am I doing that? I don't have a gun to his head."

"In a way, you do. You repeat yourself, probably a little louder each time. You tell him, 'You need to connect with me.' It's almost, 'You *have to* connect with me.' You even follow him out the door and keep at it."

"Oh, because I'm trying to keep the marriage together, now you think I'm badgering him?" (I could see part of her success in business. I would have hated to have been on the other side of the negotiating table from her.)

I said, "No, I am on your side here. I think you are truly trying to connect and get him to connect with you. What I am saying to you, however, is that you are also resisting his choices and his freedom to make his choices. And as long as he experiences that from you, he will continue to withdraw even more vigorously from you."

Beth thought about that a moment, then said, "OK, maybe I might be doing that. [I loved her certainty!] But what am I supposed to do instead?"

"When you get home, before you guys have another incident and are in a peaceful moment, say, 'I am sorry I haven't been letting you have your own choices to be connected to me. I think I might have been badgering you, and I don't blame you for withdrawing. So you are free to not talk to me about problems and stress. I won't try to make you connect with me. At the same time, I do want to be close to you and share a deeper life with you. I just wanted you to know that. I can't make you connect, but I do need you to connect.'"

I continued: "It's similar to how God treats us. He tells us He wants us to follow Him, and He tells us what He wants us to do, to have a good life and a good connection with Him. But He doesn't follow us out the door repeating Himself to us an infinite number of times."

Beth was quiet a moment. Then she said, "This is going to be really hard."

"I know," I said. "Think how God feels."

I wasn't referring to God having to apologize for anything, for He is never unloving toward us. I was referring instead to His capacity to give us freedom to choose and how difficult that must be for Him. He knows the way life should work. He knows what your best career path is. He knows what location you would thrive in the most if you lived there. He knows what relationships would be the safest and most satisfying for you. But He lets you choose all these things. Further, He is willing to allow His people to stumble and even hurt one another because He so values our freedom. And—as the rest of this chapter illustrates—His high value for freedom is born out of His love. So to understand why God allows suffering, we must first understand love and God's relationship to love.

## GOD WANTS US TO LOVE

The essence of all that God is always comes down to love. It is His nature. At His deepest level, He is love (1 John 4:16). Though He is self-sufficient in some way that we can't fathom, within the connectedness of the Father, Son, and Holy Spirit, He deeply desires a personal relationship with us. He is not satisfied with our external obedience or our rituals or our compliance. He wants a connection—one from the heart:

> Love the LORD your God with all your heart and with all your soul and with all your strength" (Deut. 6:5 NIV).

> "But I lavish unfailing love for a thousand generations on those who love me and obey my commands" (Ex. 20:6 NLT).

"I love all who love me. Those who search will surely find me" (Prov. 8:17 NLT).

"Those who accept my commandments and obey them are the ones who love me. And because they love me, my Father will love them. And I will love them and reveal myself to each of them" (John 14:21 NLT).

From the beginning of time, when He walked with Adam and Eve, God has wanted a relationship with us. And till the end of time, He wants that relationship to continue. Love is both the means and the end, in a sense. In a book I wrote called *Loving People*,[1] I set out to understand and explain how ultimately nothing God created can be more important than love. Love helps us stay together through hard times. It helps us dream of achieving better things. It keeps us alive. Love gives us hope, strength, courage, optimism, and meaning for life. A life full of love, *even in hard times,* is a good life. A life empty of love, even in good times, is a sad life.

God loves the human race deeply. But the strange reality is that He also wants and desires our love. Loving God is a major reason we were created and exist. We don't understand fully why our love for Him is so important unless, psychologically, you have a narcissistic bent and you think that God and the world must simply revolve around your specialness! But for most of humanity, it's a hard concept to wrap our thoughts around.

I became more deeply involved in my faith while I was a college student. There was a group that I met with, and they encouraged thinking and exploration when it came to biblical concepts. I had many conversations with other students about God. I read the Bible a lot and studied various authors. We had lots of arguments, debates, and late-night bull sessions. It was the freedom of the college environment to run rampant. Being somewhat of an information junkie, I was very intellectually and spiritually stimulated at this time.

At the same time, however, I had a problem with God. I loved learning the information about Him, but I was also a performance junkie. I was afraid I would let Him down, and I didn't want to bug Him with my actions. So a lot of my formative spirituality was fear-based. For me, *wanting to please God* was more important than *connecting with Him.* A perfect example would be my devotional time with God in those days. Most people use this time to pray and talk to God and read the Bible, thinking about Him and their lives. But it became a chore and an obligation for me, and I really didn't enjoy it. It was simply something to check off my list. Basically, I had a devotional life so I could avoid feeling guilty. I really didn't get a lot out of that time, except, of course, more information. So I figured that was just the way things were and would always be. That was the normal life of faith, as far as I knew.

However, sometime during my junior year, a pastor I knew began talking to me about connecting with God on a more personal and relational level. Over a couple of months of meetings, he took a group of us through some words from Jesus: "Abide in Me, and I in you. As the branch cannot bear fruit of itself, unless it abides in the vine, so neither can you, unless you abide in Me. I am the vine, you are the branches; he who abides in Me, and I in him, he bears much fruit; for apart from Me, you can do nothing" (John 15:4–5 NASB). Over the course of these meetings, he taught that more than anything, God wants us to abide with Him, and everything else good and meaningful comes from that.

Those lessons changed me on a profound and fundamental level. I related to God and to myself on a different level. I felt that I was *home.* The word *abide,* meaning "remain," had great significance for me. I experienced a tremendous gratitude and a deep sense of connection and love from God. It was as if I was able to stop trying so hard for

God and simply connect to Him. The experience changed my life to this day. And I began to learn more and more how deeply God wanted to connect with me, live in me, and have me live in Him. It was what Paul refers to as the "life of God" (Eph. 4:18 NIV), that is, a life that is based on a relationship of connection and intimacy. This is the life we were designed to have with each other and with God.

Think of a person whom you both like *and* love. You like being with her, and you love her character. When you know your lunch date with her is coming soon, you look forward to it. And when you're not around her and she comes to mind, you miss her and wonder how she is doing. It would be hard to imagine dreading that lunch date and thinking, *I'll be glad that meeting is over so I can check it off the to do list; now I won't feel guilty.* It would be an empty and disappointing experience for both of you. It is the same way with God. Even with all His other attributes, He is relational. He wants to be wanted. And He loves to be loved. He connects.

If you have had a lot of guilt or performance-based spiritual teaching, you may also find that your *fear* of God is greater than your *love* of God. This will never work in any fulfilling way for you. You will have struggles, as I have had, in moving toward Him. We certainly are to fear God, that is, have respect and awe for Him. But that fear should not keep us moving away from Him in love and relationship. He wants our love: "And now, Israel, what does the LORD your God require of you? He requires only that you fear the LORD your God, and live in a way that pleases him, and love him and serve him with all your heart and soul" (Deut. 10:12 NLT).

## WE ARE FREE TO BE UNLOVING

God has constructed love and relationships with a requirement, and that is freedom. Freedom is the price tag of love. Freedom exists in the service of love, for love can't be forced. It can't be controlled. It can't be coerced. It can't be intimidated or threatened. It is impossible to *should* love. That is an oxymoron. Basically, when we feel we *have to* love someone, we have erased the possibility of love. We can only love God—and, for that matter, anyone else—when we have a choice and are completely free to walk, free to say, "I'm out of this relationship," free to put God out of our minds and our lives. That is not a pleasant thought, but there is a law of relationships here. Simply stated, it is this: *we are not free to love unless we are free not to love.* If you don't have a choice, you cannot freely move toward God—or any person.

The Bible never says you *have to* follow God because you don't. He treats you like an adult. He wants a free choice or none at all. He wants you to choose or not choose Him: "But if you refuse to serve the LORD, then choose today whom you will serve" (Josh. 24:15 NLT). It is a little astounding when you think about it. God gives up all the control He could use and puts Himself in an extremely humble and vulnerable position. He asks us to love Him and follow Him. And He waits for us to make up our minds. What a dilemma that puts God in! He certainly has the power and wherewithal to force the issue. He could reach inside your heart and tweak it so that you wouldn't have a choice to turn from Him. But He doesn't do that because He wants to be pursued. He will give back many times more than He will ever receive from us, but He does want to be wanted.

We make confused choices when we act out of our fears, our baggage, our egos, or any number of sinful motives. And though God often tells us to change our ways, He allows us to choose what is not best. He allows us to go our own way. In God's mind, if you make the free choice to walk away from Him, that is preferable to a coerced or manipulated choice to walk toward Him. He has an extremely high value for your freedom. You can see this in Jesus' words as He describes the three stances we can take toward His love: "I know all the things you do, that you are neither hot nor cold. I wish that you were one or the other!

But since you are like lukewarm water, neither hot nor cold, I will spit you out of my mouth!" (Rev. 3:15–16 NLT). This is a remarkable statement. God prefers cold rejection to our being lukewarm toward Him. That is an unusual way to look at relationships.

Have you ever had a love relationship in which someone you cared about deeply may have been with you but was not really interested in you? It is a painful experience. Most of us would ultimately rather be without that person than be in a relationship where we do not have the whole heart of the one we desire. This passage illustrates the value of freedom: God would rather us wholeheartedly love Him—or wholeheartedly hate Him—than for us to be stuck in the middle. The cold person at least is sure of something and committed to it. That means if he ever decides to follow God, he will most likely become hot and jump right in. But the lukewarm person may stay apathetic forever. And the source of much of the lukewarm problem is *a lack of freedom*. The lukewarm person doesn't feel sure enough to make a commitment, right or wrong. He fears that he will make the wrong choice. In the singles world, it's the commitment-phobic person who is terrified of marriage. In the work world, it's the talented person who can't find her niche and can't commit to any area of expertise, choosing to be a jack-of-all-trades and giving up depth of focus. Some internal conflict renders the individual frozen and unable to make bold or risky moves.

Think about a relationship in which you have struggled—perhaps in your marriage or in a friendship with a child or family member. And while you care about the other person, they are alienated from you and are withdrawing. You can't reach them, so to speak. You can't get to their heart, to the connection. What would you do? Would you actually take the step of saying, "You *have to* love me. You *have to* spend time with me. Even if your heart is far from me, you *have to* be with me." Of course, you would not. That would be empty. It would not give you what you are wanting and needing from that relationship. No one wants to have someone spend time with them because he or she has to or should. No woman wants a man to ask her out to dinner, make a commitment, even marry her while all the time inside his heart, he is wishing he were somewhere else. She wants him to want her, to desire her, to look forward to being with her, to miss her, to think about her in positive ways. You don't want to be what they called in high school the *charity date*. That has no value. I know, I have been a charity date, and it is no fun!

Beth, my corporate friend, couldn't make Josh move toward her. Josh must be able to freely choose if he wants her or not. That doesn't mean she can't ask, influence, take ownership of her part of the problem, and so on. Certainly she should do all those things. But she ultimately must allow Josh to be free to move away from her if he is ever going to choose to move toward her.

And that is how God feels and how He approaches us. Beth was frustrated and felt somewhat powerless that Josh was avoidant and nonresponsive to taking ownership. Multiply that by some huge factor, and that is closer to God's experience. All He would have to do is make us obey, and then we would not hurt ourselves. But He doesn't.

At the same time, He has feelings about this. It hurts Him. God is not detached or disconnected emotionally from this conflict. He feels the anguish any parent does when a child makes bad choices. And He talks about His feelings:

> Oh, how can I give you up, Israel?
>> How can I let you go?
> How can I destroy you like Admah
>> or demolish you like Zeboiim?
> My heart is torn within me,
>> and my compassion overflows.
> —Hosea 11:8 (NLT)

It's hard to imagine the depth of His emotions here. He is literally in conflict over His people. And yet, He does not force us to behave or to clean up our world.

To live in an atmosphere of freedom is the only way you will ever love God or anyone and the only way anyone will ever truly love you. I have seen that freedom work in my life and the lives of many others as well, with the end result being that people grew to a place where they could love God fully, completely, and with all their hearts. For example, a friend of mine was very angry with God over her divorce and how her and her kids' lives were turned upside down as a result. She didn't disbelieve in God's existence. In fact, it would have been easier for her if He didn't exist. She felt that He had let her down in a major way and had caused her great harm. She stopped going to church, praying, reading her Bible, and all the other things she'd once done to relate to God. This happened for several months. God didn't strike her with lightning or tell her how disappointed He was in her. From her report, He didn't do anything but wait. Finally, she told me that *she began missing God.* She missed the connection and the love she felt from Him and His presence. And gradually, she began to enter the spiritual activities and disciplines she had been involved in, and she reconnected with Him. She had been free to not love God, so she didn't for awhile. And that freedom gave her the space to experience a lack of relationship with God. She freely moved away. And then she freely moved toward Him again. As she tells it, the past few years since all that happened have been the deepest and most meaningful times with God in her life.

The process of parenting also illustrates this spiritual principle in relational terms. Barbi and I are parents of two teens. The adolescent years are the season of de-parenting. It's the time when the kids are moving away from home and launching into their friends and outside lives. They have less and less investment in the family nest. The driver's license was the big tipping point for us. Once they were mobile, we noticed a dramatic shift in their schedules and interest in us! We are just not on their radar as much, and that is how it should be. Barbi and I try to do what all parents should do during these years—keep the family connected, allow the appropriate freedoms, monitor both the home world and the outside world, and so forth. But the reality is, kids are less and less involved with their parents as they get older. It's not because they are angry at us or don't like us. It is simply the developmental process of "leaving and cleaving" (Gen. 2:24).

But Barbi and I do miss them, and we notice the times without them more. We are sad but still glad they are moving on in life. We're trying to stay on track with the program God developed for them. However, the other day I drove home after work and was lying on the bed for a few minutes, taking a power nap before dinner. In my twilight state, I heard Benny, our younger son, walk in the house. Normally he would go to his room or the kitchen or the computer area. My bedroom is outside of his normal path. So I figured when I got up, I'd go down and find him and say hi. But all of a sudden he walked into the room, plopped on the bed beside me, and began talking about his day.

I was so happy! Here, this independent-minded seventeen-year-old high-school upperclassman, developing a life on his own, had gone out of his way to be with me. I had this joyful emotion that my son wanted to hang out with me. It was wonderful. I'll keep that memory and others similar to it. I think that is a little of how God feels when we look for Him when we don't have to love Him but simply do. It is a joy and is worth a great deal.

## THE MISUSE OF FREEDOM

Freedom is a hefty price tag for God's desire to be loved. It has cost Him, and it has cost us, dearly. Freedom means that God allows us to walk away from Him and His ways, and He allows people to misuse that freedom and hurt other people. We are free in all sorts of ways:

- People can become drunk and swerve their car into a family minivan.
- Spouses can criticize and abuse their mates.
- Singles can be unkind to someone they are dating.
- Parents can think more of their own comfort than the good of their kids.
- Third World dictators are free to oppress their people.
- Bosses can exploit the talents of their employees and then lay them off with no loyalty.
- Financial experts can use their freedom to contribute to a global economic crash.

The list could go on and on. And this is where we often get stuck. It is where our where-is-God questions often arise. A good God allows people to be destructive? How can that be? Are those things on that list supposed to be seen as wonderful? No. No one in their right mind would ever say they are good. They are not; they are terrible and horribly hurtful. But they are a consequence of our freedom. They are what happens when people use their choices to be as unloving as they can be. You may have been the recipient of someone's freedom to be unloving. You may have suffered greatly at the hands of, in the influence of, or under the control of someone who did not treat you in a loving way. And the unfair part of it is, as I mentioned in the last chapter, that your duty is to forgive and heal, not to extract vengeance, though it may be justified. That is not an easy thing to say, but it is the reality: "Instead, be kind to each other, tenderhearted, forgiving one another, just as God through Christ has forgiven you" (Eph. 4:32 NLT).

# THE HIGH PRICE OF LOVE

So the only conclusion I can reach is that love must be worth a great deal to God because it comes at a very, very high price. It must be indeed precious to Him. God allows things to go wrong in terrible, terrible ways because He wants people to love Him and one another from our hearts and not from force. Still, it's a hard concept. A friend once asked me over dinner, "Why couldn't God have come up with a better idea? If He is God, why couldn't He have set the laws of life so that we can love Him and yet not be free to be cruel to each other?" I suppose He could do that if He wanted. He could suspend the laws of gravity and electromagnetism also, but He doesn't. Truthfully, the idea of freedom in the service of love simply makes sense. We all want love. We all want a choice in who we love. That's the only way I can imagine that relationships will ever work, which brings us full circle.

Let me summarize all this in four simple points:

1. God desires for humanity to love Him.
2. For love to be real, people must be free to not love Him.
3. People misuse that freedom and hurt each other.
4. That freedom shows how high a price the value of love is.

I hope that this idea about freedom does not make you think that God is detached from all of this. He doesn't just stand by and watch impassively while you lose your job or your marriage, saying, "Oh well, it's about freedom. It's about choice. Too bad for you. Welcome to my system of ordering the universe." I don't think that is what the Bible teaches at all. He is not disconnected at all but very involved. In fact, a great deal of this book explains His involvement when we hurt, especially in chapter 7 about God's suffering with us. As we will see,

He has deep feelings about our experiences. But He doesn't violate freedom. Remember that if He is willing for us to endure suffering from each others' hands to the extent that He does, how much then does He value and want our love to be real and authentic.

# CHAPTER 5

# THE GOD YOU MUST NOT SEEK

A friend of mine who is struggling in his career said today, when I asked him to go to church with me, "So I'm a project for you?" His response is a good example of something that needs to be cleared up, early in the game: some of you simply may not be asking where God is. In times of trouble and difficulty, you may be hesitant to find Him. You may not feel free to seek Him with all your heart, soul, and mind. You may want to avoid God or may feel hostile to him. You may even simply be dismissing Him as irrelevant. Whatever the case, you may be spending little time and energy in searching for His help and grace.

This is an important psychological and spiritual dynamic, and it is more common than we realize. There is a god who, in reality, you should not seek. He will not be a source of presence or power for you. He will neither provide for you nor give you answers. He will always let you down. Though He may be quite familiar to you, He is to be avoided at all costs. This is the god who has been forged out of painful emotional and relational experiences. *But He is not the real God.* He is a mass of mental distortions. And you need to understand your internal picture of God and how to deal with it if you have any desire to clear the way for the One who is for you in your hard circumstances. There is not room for both, and the actual God must win this round. We will deal with several false versions of God that people struggle with:

- ANGRY GOD: How do you feel safe with Him?
- UNPLEASABLE GOD: You might as well just give up.
- DISCONNECTED GOD: He is unavailable.
- INDULGENT GOD: There are no rules to protect you.

We are not a people who perceive reality as it truly is 100 percent of the time. Our internal "lens" fogs up and distorts what is going on. And it generally defaults toward the negative, not the positive. For example, suppose someone you know leaves you a voice mail that says, "Call me. I need to talk to you." Nothing more, just that. If this is a new relationship, if it is a person you are having trouble with, or if you have had a really stressful day, odds are high you will think, *He is angry with me. He is going to come down on me for something I did.* You'll dread the call-back and perhaps even avoid it. Your dread may be correct: you may be facing a difficult conversation. But it's just as likely that the person has a problem he wants your help with or even that he just wants to talk to you. It probably isn't the best voice mail etiquette, but it happens. We fill in the blanks with false assumptions about how the person feels about us. And the result is that we do not want contact with the individual. We have little longing or desire for connection. At our best, we call because we want to do the right thing by facing an issue and solving a problem. But we certainly don't look forward to it and think, *I wonder what he wants? This will be a good conversation!* And that creates a problem. It is no way to approach a relationship of love. Duty and obligation are important, but if the only reason you spend time with someone is duty and obligation, something is not as it should be.

Just as with the voice mail example, we try to avoid God when we have problems. His design is that He be the first place we run to: "Search for the LORD and for his strength; continually seek him" (Ps. 105:4 NLT). But when we possess psychological distortions of His care and nature, this process of seeking is handicapped and hampered. Some idea or image of Him and how He would respond to your situation prohibits the search. The consequence is that we often do not fully and thoroughly look for God in the dark times. We end up alone or, at best, with some weak help-me prayer. We believe the source of our hope is someone who is not entirely safe for us.

I was consulting with Ross, a businessman who was going through a difficult time financially. He had been very successful but had made some errors in judgment about some investments and had lost a great deal of money. Part of this was his fault, part was the advice he was receiving, and part was a difficult market in general. But it was a serious blow to him and his family, and they were struggling. He was very discouraged and was trying to work his way back to a point of financial stability. He had been a Christian for a long time, and the subject of our conversation turned to his faith. He mentioned that he had not really put a significant amount of time into praying about his situation. I asked him about that, knowing that he was a person who was devoted to his spiritual life.

He said, "I think I'm avoiding God on this problem."

I asked him, "That doesn't sound like you. Why would that be?"

He blurted out, as if it was on the tip of his tongue, "I think He's mad at me." There was a little silence while we looked at each other, and his words hung in the air between us.

Then he quickly backtracked and said, "I didn't mean it that way. I know He loves me."

But I intervened: "Wait a minute, Ross. You meant something here. I know you know God loves you, at least intellectually, and probably mostly emotionally as well. But it is possible that, in some circumstances, you may not be very sure of that?"

He said, "But He has taken such good care of me and my family."

I said, "Yes. He has. But this isn't about Him or His care. Do you wonder how He feels when you make significant mistakes, at least in the moment you think about it, before your intellect comes up with the right answer."

Ross reflected and said, "Yeah, when I screw up, for a second I think the axe is going to fall, but then I recover and I know He is on my side."

I said, "Right. There is a part of you that sees God as mad at your mistakes, but that is uncomfortable . . . as it would be for me. So your intellect talks you out of it . . . until the next time you fail."

It became a very helpful conversation, one that landed where we didn't expect. Ross began to see how he had always seen God as angry when he did something wrong. Therefore, he tried not to make mistakes and certainly didn't spend a lot of time in prayer about his mistakes, where he could have gotten some relief. Not only that, but on a psychological level, Ross could not be creative and a risk-taker, able to screw up and learn from it. Who can do that when the axe is about to fall?

## THE ALTERNATIVES

If you can identify with Ross, you can identify with having some hesitation in taking your hard times to God. It's an image we carry, and it is not an accurate picture of the One who is for us. My experience of people who have distorted perceptions of God is that they each approach Him in a different way.

Some bring only their praises and thanks to Him and don't want to talk about their failures. They have a sort of compulsion to always look at the bright side and be happy for the victories. When they bring up their hurts, they minimize the pain and maximize God's care: *God, I know I was laid off, and this is great! What an opportunity to see you do a miracle.* I believe that is true, that it is an opportunity for a miracle. But if there was no process of honesty about the problem prior to that, I tend to wonder if the person is avoiding bringing bad news to God. Remember that the Israelites, the chosen people, were in the wilderness for forty years before actually experiencing the Promised Land. They had some hard times and suffering before they entered the land. We don't always have positive experiences all the time, even though God is in charge, and we should not pretend otherwise.

Alternatively, some people will guilt themselves and see God as righteously punishing them: *God, I know I was laid off, and this is what I get for not working hard enough.* Again, sure, we have consequences when we don't take responsibility for our lives. But if that is all I hear, I suspect a harsh and angry image of God at work in the person's mind.

The other response I notice is despair. People avoid the search and the seeking. They don't expect a good thing to happen. They expect bad things or nothing at all, so they despair of God's provision and try to go it alone. This is sad, and it happens often. It is not who God is or what He is about.

## THE DISTORTIONS

In my experience working with people, the God they should not seek occurs in several fairly distinct patterns—the ones I mentioned briefly at the beginning of the chapter. Often, individuals have a combination of these as well.

## THE ANGRY GOD

This distorted image of God is that He is mad at you. As in Ross's example, this often happens when you fail. There is a trigger that occurs when you make a mistake, intentional or unintentional. You believe God is pleased when you do well and bugged when you foul up. He can be mildly irritated with your actions. In some cases, He can be enraged and condemning toward you. For some, this is a constant state. No matter what they do, He is irritated. Even their successes don't appease His anger. Though they know in their heads that they are reconciled to him through Jesus (2 Cor. 5:18), they do not feel or experience this reality. So in hard times, the first thing they say is, "I'm in trouble with God." In some more severe cases, I have worked with people who actually perceived God's anger as mean and abusive. In their minds, in some sick way, God took pleasure in punishing them. What a horrible spiritual relationship! The God we are to turn to in hard times is the One who will hurt us more. Who would seek Him for this response? That is a road to fear, not to love.

## THE UNPLEASABLE GOD

You can never do enough, try hard enough, or be good enough to make this God happy. He has created a list of rules that you can never completely fulfill. You spend your time and energy trying to get it right, but He is critical and disappointed in you, no matter what. Your 99 percent is not enough. Can you see how this would be a devastating God to relate to in a health crisis or marriage dysfunction? No matter how hard you search, ask, and try to fix the problem, the struggle is happening because of something you missed. In a karmic way, you didn't get it right. You didn't say the right thing, ask the right question, or try the right medical procedure. Though you understand, theologically, that he does not base His love on your performance because the Law has been fulfilled in Christ—"And because you belong to him, the power of the life-giving Spirit has freed you from the power of sin that leads to death" (Rom. 8:2 NLT)—that's not how it feels inside. The Bible's reality is compartmentalized in some file folder in your mind, but it is not an experience in your heart.

## THE DISCONNECTED GOD

You may see God as detached and uninvolved with your situation. He sits on His throne and leaves you twisting in the wind. He is not angry, wrathful, or displeased. He is just not there—not emotionally or with any real help. He may care for you in some official, legal sense, but His care doesn't really make any difference in the long run. As in the angry-God distortion, the uninvolvement can be a constant state, where you see Him as a cosmic Being who watches dispassionately and philosophically and lets the universe wind down toward its final end. Some, however, see Him more as being so preoccupied with the "big" issues of life that their personal situation doesn't register on God's radar: *He has entire continents that are in real need of His help; I'm just being selfish.* People with this distortion don't often experience the reality of Jesus' words of reassurance:

> What is the price of two sparrows—one copper coin? But not a single sparrow can fall to the ground without your Father knowing it. And the very hairs on your head are all numbered. So don't be afraid; you are more valuable to God than a whole flock of sparrows.
> —Matthew 10:29–31 (NLT)

## THE INDULGENT GOD

Here is a distortion on the positive end of things rather than the negative. Some people experience God as a Being who is so full of grace that He winks at our selfishness, dismisses our hurtfulness, and overlooks our irresponsibility. That is, God, having been reconciled to us through Christ, is pretty much happy about everything we do. People who have this distortion will often think as they contemplate some destructive decision ahead of them, *He'll forgive me, so it's OK.* Or *I don't have to be concerned about making mistakes because I'm under grace.* So in difficult circumstances, individuals who believe in this God wreak havoc in their lives and those around them. They tend to blame others and act on impulse without regard to future consequences, and as a result, people get hurt. They have often had a lifetime of little truth, structure, consequences, or requirements for them to be responsible. So they have no real template for a healthy concern for their effect on others.

I once counseled a man who had this psychological bent. He was unfaithful to his wife. She was devastated and understandably so. Her entire world had been shattered. When she and I talked to him about it, his response was that she should understand that God forgave him, and she should too. She was devastated again, and I was very discouraged with his answer. It was a true but incomplete theological statement on his part. It did not take all of God's character into consideration. God did forgive him. And she had a responsibility to forgive. But this woman needed great healing as well, and she needed much remorse, change, care, and humility from him. His God did not see it that way, however, and they eventually divorced. She could not take the prospect that she was in jeopardy of it happening again with the attitude he had.

Certainly God is full of grace, and certainly God will forgive. That is what He is about. But this mental distortion misses the reality that God also is righteous and holy and does not put up with evil, sin, and hurtfulness:

> I will reject perverse ideas
>> and stay away from every evil.
> I will not tolerate people who slander their neighbors.

50

I will not endure conceit and pride.

—Psalm 101:4–5 (NLT)

God knows hard times come. He knows we fail, and often we contribute to our own suffering. He wants to help us change, repent, learn, and grow. The Indulgent God, however, is not that way. Basically, he substitutes license for grace. Everything is OK under grace in this distortion. But in reality, while everything can be forgiven, that never makes hurtfulness OK.

There are other sorts of psychological distortions, but these are the ones I see the most in counseling, speaking, and my radio work. There are other good sources of information about these issues that are worth reading about (for example, read Juanita Ryan's article "Seeing God in New Ways: Recovery from Distorted Images of God," National Association of Christian Recovery, www.nacronline.com).

When I encounter these distortions, I feel a curious empathy for God as well as for the individuals who suffer from them. I think about how much He wants to relate to us, how much effort He goes to, and how much He reaches out to us in order to help us connect: "I will walk among you; I will be your God, and you will be my people" (Lev. 26:12 NLT). Imagine what it must be like for God to care so much and do all He does, only to have us shrink back from Him in fear, avoid Him, resent Him, or simply misunderstand Him. It cannot be easy to be the real God, competing with all the emotional distortions of Him and often having to let us walk away from Him. If you have ever been made the bad guy in a relationship, with the other person being stuck seeing you as someone you are not, no matter what you did, that is probably some sliver of identification with God's experience. He has a deep desire to be truly known, that is, understood and loved, for Himself, in full reality and clarity. The day will come when this happens, but it is not here yet:

And they will not need to teach their neighbors,
>    nor will they need to teach their relatives,
>    saying, "You should know the LORD."
> For everyone, from the least to the greatest,
>    will know me already.
—Hebrews 8:11 (NLT)

# THE SOURCES

The point is, these God-distortions are simply bad for everyone involved. If you have them, you need to deal with them. It's important to understand that we don't make these distortions up out of thin air. They come from somewhere, and it helps to see their origins.

The problem of seeing Him as a Being He is not first began with Adam and Eve. When they disobeyed God by eating the forbidden fruit, a strange thing happened to them. They experienced the universe's first emotion of fear. They became afraid. God asked Adam where he was, and "He replied, 'I heard you walking in the garden, so I hid. I was afraid because I was naked'" (Gen. 3:10 NLT). Why would they be afraid of God? They knew He loved them and was their source of life. Why did they not call out and ask Him for His help and grace in their situation, their own "difficult times"? Adam and Eve's sin had a unique effect on them. It certainly alienated and disconnected them from God, as we all understand. But another thing happened as well. That disconnection caused them to be filled with self-condemnation and fear of God's wrath instead of His love. I believe that this is because *in the absence of relationship, we experience condemnation.* When we do not feel grace, love, and care from God or from another person, the void within us does not stay empty; it does not stay in neutral. Instead, we are filled with self-judgment and also the fear of God's judgment.

Here's another way to express it: loss of connection leads to the presence of guilt feelings. This is true psychologically in relationships. When people are isolated or disconnected from letting others into their vulnerabilities because of old injuries, trust issues, or hurts, they often experience themselves as "bad" and have a good deal of negative, critical self-talk. They beat up on themselves and expect others to judge them harshly as well. And the same thing occurs spiritually—on the vertical level—with God. So the parents of the human race created the first "God you should not seek," the God of their mental distortions. I have written about this issue in more depth in another book, *Hiding from Love*.[1]

There is an emotional aspect to the causes of distortions about God as well. They often occur when there is a significant problem in a significant personal relationship. It is important to understand that our image of God, whom we can't see, is deeply affected by people, whom we can see. Our significant relationships tint our entire outlook on life. If we have been surrounded by love, structure, and health, we will tend to have a realistic and positive view of life. That principle was designed to work for our good and even to turn us toward God. God designed us to learn of His trustworthiness and care from other people. Babies learn from a loving and safe mother that God is safe: "Yet you brought me safely from my mother's womb and led me to trust you at my mother's breast" (Ps. 22:9 NLT). The human connection prepares us for the eternal connection.

However, the converse can happen as well with damaging results. If there are relational hurts and wounds, we may have a negative and distorted view of God, people, and life. We learn from human relationships that people can be safe, kind, and caring or that they can be selfish and destructive. Who has not experienced someone being hurtful to them and then being somewhat hesitant about opening up to someone else?

We are talking about *emotional baggage* here. Past hurts that aren't healed will stay with us in the present, and they affect the way we look at everything. The baggage of emotional detachment, abandonment, control, condemnation, or shame, among others, can seriously distort how you look at and experience God's love and care.

For example, a friend of mine told me her story about God and hard times. Her tough circumstance was a very difficult divorce. There were terrible custody and financial battles that tore everyone up. This qualified as a situation in which she certainly needed to seek out God and His help. However, she had grown up in a family whose central figure was a domineering and harsh dad. He kept his wife and kids terrified of His anger. She learned to be compliant, to withdraw, and never to say what she felt. She saw what happened to her brothers when someone spoke up, and it was very hurtful to her. Not knowing she was doing it, my friend began to see her heavenly Father through the lens of her earthly father. God seemed condemning and dangerous to her. She had faith but not the kind that allowed her to make a deep emotional connection with God.

Flashing forward, then, to her divorce: in her time of desperation and great need, she wanted to pour her heart out to God so that she would not be alone and so that she could gain strength and help from him. However, it did not happen. Her need to express her pain, her loss, her unhappiness, her fear, and her anger at her situation, which also included negative feelings toward God ("Why are you allowing this misery?"), were prohibited by her terror that God would judge her for being so honest. So she could not go to Him. It was a tough position to be in, living through a crisis and trying to find answers but being so restricted from a deep and emotionally authentic connection with God. Fortunately, she realized what was going on and went to work on the injuries. She found a competent Christian therapist, and over time, as she healed from her dad's influence, she began to enter into a much better relationship with God.

She found His love and care, not just intellectually but emotionally, as His role as her heavenly father began to clarify itself: "Father to the fatherless, defender of widows—this is God, whose dwelling is holy" (Ps. 68:5 NLT).

## KEEPING A BALANCE

Over the years, I have seen how the power of a distorted view of God operates, time and time again, through the lens of significant relationships. It is extremely helpful to understand this concept and how greatly it affects our connection and perception of God. However, sometimes people oversimplify the nature of the emotional baggage and reach the wrong conclusions about the God-distortion problem. It is important to keep a balanced perspective here. For example, an individual will say something like, "You will relate to God the same way you related to your father." If Dad was distant, so is God. If he was rigid, so is God, and so forth. There is much more to this issue than that one-to-one correspondence. The distortion is from significant relationships of all types, not just fathers but also mothers, siblings, friends, spouses, and relatives.

It's worth noting that we sometimes react with an opposite perspective than the experience our hurtful relationships have taught us. For example, I had a client who came from a chaotic, alcoholic family background where he experienced a great deal of emotional damage. God truly became his anchor away from his family relationships, and he experienced God as safe, stable, and protective—God's true character—in contrast to the unreliable and dangerous personalities of his parents. As the Psalms illustrate: "Keep me safe, O God, for I have come to you for refuge" (Ps. 16:1 NLT). My client's healing and recovery process was accelerated through his relationship with God.

# BREAKING THROUGH THE MESS

On our third day out from Argentina, moving past the Drake Passage on the way to Antarctica, I was in my room when I heard a loud grinding sound and felt the ship slow down and begin to vibrate. The engines were operating at a lower gear. When I arrived at the deck, I saw that we were in the middle of a sea ice area where, for miles around, the surface of the ocean was frozen over. Though we were slowing down, the ship, being an icebreaker, started cutting through the ice slowly and methodically. We had ice in front, in back, and on both sides. We continued for miles, breaking up the ice and moving on. This experience was a metaphor for our relationship with God in light of our emotional baggage. If your baggage from the past has distorted your ability to feel safe and open to God, you need to begin cutting through the mess and clearing it out.

This is such an important idea, especially in how much we need to find the true God in the hard times we're facing these days. We are all in need of who He really is. All of us, at some level, do well to investigate if we need to clean out the cup (Matt. 23:26), take a look inside, and see how we perceive God and how that perception measures up to His real character. Having done that, we are able to reorient our distorted image to one closer to His real nature. Here are some steps that can move you down that path.

## PRAY FOR CLARITY

Ask God, "Are there ways I experience You that do not reflect who You really are?" God, above all, is motivated to be known by you. He doesn't want some distortion to clutter up the connection. He will help you to clear up the mess. Sometimes I will have people pray through Psalm 139:23–24:

Search me, O God, and know my heart;
Try me and know my anxious thoughts;

And see if there be any hurtful way in me,

And lead me in the everlasting way (NASB).

Wait a while, pay attention, and record any impressions you might get from that prayer.

## IDENTIFY WHAT YOU SEE FROM YOUR EXPERIENCE

Start with the distortions we've covered in this chapter: angry, unpleasable, disconnected, indulgent. As I mentioned, you may experience God as being something other than one of these. If you don't identify with any of these or think that your mind has other distortions in addition to these, write the other ones you are aware of.

Sometimes it helps to launch your thoughts with a few open phrases like these:

- When I need God's help in my current hard situation, I expect Him to feel _____ toward me.

- When I fail and make a bad decision, I think God feels _____ with me.

- When I try my best and still struggle, I expect Him to feel _____ toward me.

- When I intentionally do wrong and am self-serving, I think He feels _____ toward me.

There are no right and wrong answers here, of course. As a psychologist, I find that these steps help impressions that you may not be aware of to come to the surface and become useful to you, a little like Ross's surprising outburst: "I think He's mad at me . . ." You may find words come to mind, such as *compassionate, supportive, gracious, empathetic,* and *patient*. Then again, you may come up with others that are darker, such as *fed up, impatient, critical, condemning,* and *uncaring.* In whatever way this happens, get your list together.

## CONNECT THE DOTS

These impressions come from somewhere, and they are most likely related to significant relationships in your past or present, as I mentioned earlier. Tie the distortions to these relationships as they come to mind, and record them as possibilities:

- The anger I feel God has toward me may come from my relationship with _____, where I was the object of a lot of wrath.

- I get afraid of God's anger because _____ avoided any confrontations with me, so I always suspect anger is lurking behind his/her smile.

- The unpleasability I expect from God may come from how _____ and I related, where I could never get it right for him/her.

- I see God as unpleasable, and I remember how things with _____ were so chaotic that I had to do all the work to keep things together, causing me to wonder if I'd ever do enough.

- My view of God as disconnected may relate to my experiences with _____, where I couldn't get enough care and attention.

- I see God as indulgent, with no requirements or consequences for me, a lot like _____ and I have related, where I didn't receive sufficient truth or structure from him/her.

These are just a few thoughts, but use them to gain perspective. You may be concerned that this is all becoming a blame game and that you are shifting responsibility onto people you care about, and what good will that do? That is not the purpose here. It is a way to understand the origins and causes of your God distortions so you can realign and correct how you perceive Him, that He may again be "a stronghold in times of trouble" (Ps. 9:9 NASB) for you during your hard times. The object is not to shift responsibility but the reverse: *to take responsibility for the distortions*, which gives you power over them.

## FORGIVE AND HEAL

While this process is not about blame, it may unearth a need for you to cancel a debt, which is the meaning of forgiveness, and also heal from some sort of relational damage. It may be minor, moderate, or severe, but it's likely that you have experienced emotional injury. This stands to reason. If a relationship was significant enough to you that it actually colored and changed how you view the nature of God, that is no small matter. Often, we will experience others, not just God, in the same distorted ways, and it can affect marriage, dating, friendship, family, and work relationships. You may want to get into a healthy small group or find a spiritual director, mentor, or therapist who can help you move past what you have experienced. The goal is to be a more whole person and to also be confident that you are approaching God as He really is, to avail yourself of all the resources He has for you, to help your present difficulty.

## STUDY GOD

God has made Himself knowable through the Bible. There are many references in Scripture to His grace, His patience, His compassion, and His righteousness. As you read and meditate on these as part of the process, they will help you to understand and experience Him for who He is. There are also some very good books that systematically describe the various attributes of God (A. W. Tozer's *Attributes of God* and J. I. Packer's *Knowing God* are two good examples). Also, new and thoughtful writers such as Donald Miller (*Blue Like Jazz*) are providing a deeply personal way of understanding God's nature in their writings. Be aware, however, that simply reading these books will most likely not be enough, especially if you have experienced significant relational struggle. When you study areas of holiness and righteousness, it may be easy to feel condemned and unloved by God. That is not the fault of these books. It is more likely that the material is triggering old wounds. Make sure that you are talking to people who are safe and on your side so that you can discuss the impressions you have and resolve them.

# CHAPTER 6

# A HOPE MORE THAN WISHING

Y ou and I need hope in God. Hope is one of the most powerful agents we have available to us in times like these. It can be simply defined as *the anticipation of a future good that we do not now experience.* Hope helps us hold on and not give in to despair, even if we don't see the positive evidence we desire to see. Hope motivates, inspires, and focuses us in our work and efforts. Hope keeps a parent consulting with doctor after doctor, searching for the specialist who can help her child. Hope moves a businessman to make phone call after phone call, to network exhaustively to find a new position after a layoff. Hope influences a single person to stay in circulation, even after relationship disappointments and heartbreak. Hope motivates a person who has lost his mate to continue his daily routine and his close friendships. The value of hope can't be overestimated. With hope, *we endure the now in anticipation of a better future.* My desire in writing this book is that if you come away with only one thing from reading it, it would be an increased sense of hope. There are few insurmountable obstacles for people who have a deep hope that is real and substantive. In that sense, the answers to the where-is-God question are designed ultimately to provide hope.

## HOPE THAT DOES NOT HELP

Not all hope is good for us or can really sustain us. Just like empty calories will leave you hungry a few minutes after eating, there are kinds of hope that don't deliver what they promise. Here are some of the kinds of unhelpful hope you'll encounter in life.

### FALSE HOPE

Hope is so important when we're facing difficult trials that sometimes we grasp for a hope that isn't real just to have something positive to hold on to. We will hear someone assure us that things are going to be OK, even if they have no basis for saying that other than wanting us to feel better, and we do feel some relief. At least that reassurance pulled us out of our funk and despair for awhile. But this is false hope, and it functions somewhat like an antidepressant. It lifts us up and even energizes us; however, when it proves to be false, it can leave us worse off than we were before. Desperate wishing can inadvertently put words based on our wishes in God's mouth, but these promises are not real and can leave us with a genuine sense of disappointment in God.

For example, a friend of mine, who was facing a terminal illness, was told by a Christian that she would be healed. That person said she had heard from God about my friend, and it was going to happen. Her family, of course, gained hope and encouragement, and life became better for awhile. There are times when I have seen recovery like this happen, a true medical miracle. But, sadly, I have seen more cases in which, over time, sickness has taken the lives of my friends.

The disappointment, confusion, and, worst of all, the doubt in God's love that would remain in the family members' minds was devastating. They sometimes felt set up by God, or, at best, that they were crashing after their well-meaning friend's "sugar high" of false hope.

Sometimes the energy people gain from false hope will help them find an unexpected solution to a problem. For example, a man who loses his position at work may believe that he is destined to work in the same industry he was in. That may not be God's plan for him, but he works very hard at networking, connecting, and being assertive in his efforts. He doesn't land in the same sector, but all his energy did lead him to something in another area that was good. So there is a sometimes positive end to false hope. However, I think it's much better to get the energy from true hope and not have to suffer the disappointment and questioning that comes afterward.

Psychologically, there is another type of problem hope called *defensive hope*. It is emotional in nature and sometimes leads to believing in false hope. With defensive hope, a person wants something to be true so badly and so deeply that she bypasses the evidence and reality and looks only toward the positive. It is a denial of what is based on need and desire. You see this often in people who have an addict in their lives. The addict uses, goes crazy, causes all sorts of damage, then promises never to use again. The family, not wanting to live in the nightmare again, believes the promises. And when the addict drops out of counseling and his recovery program, saying he doesn't need it and he's strong enough now, the family believes him. And when he uses again and crashes, promising afterward that he'll never do it gain for sure, the family believes him.

This hope is defensive because the family is defending itself against what is true, which is that the addict is not in the program and, therefore, has very little chance of staying clean and sober. Conversely, true hope believes in what is real. If the addict were saying, "I hate what I am doing to myself and to my family so much that I'm willing to go to treatment until they say I'm done," that would give them real hope for his recovery. Though he is still using, I would have hope for that person because I see a seed of hunger and need and honesty inside him. But if he is clean for a few weeks with no treatment and looks OK, I don't ever have much hope. Like false hope, defensive hope is based on our wishes for things to be better with no foundation in reality.

## HOPELESSNESS

Hopelessness is the state in which we feel there are no good options, no good future, and nothing positive to anticipate. Tomorrow seems as if it will be no better than today, and so do all the other tomorrows, day after day after day. Hopelessness can cause severe life problems. It can lead to helplessness, giving up, acting out, despair, and losing one's faith in God. The absence of hope in your life can cause your heart to weaken and become sick: "Hope deferred makes the heart sick, but a dream fulfilled is a tree of life" (Prov. 13:12 NLT). It is a hard state of being.

I have experienced hopelessness in my life as probably everyone has. After I graduated from college, I moved about fifteen hundred miles away from my home and began working at a children's home. I was a twenty-three-year-old cottage parent for seven teenage boys. Needless to say, it was a very difficult situation for both me and the boys. There was constant chaos, impulsivity, violence, and confusion. There are some people who did great work in this role, but I was not one of them. I just didn't have the maturity or life skills to mentor these boys. I hope today that those boys have recovered from my working with them! So I lasted about a year and a half, and I finally quit the job because I simply couldn't continue. I had no job, no income, no prospects, and I was living several states away from my family and friends. It was one of the worst periods in my life, a real time of hope-lessness. In fact, I became depressed, and it took a while for that to be resolved.

Having said that, I would still take the discomfort of hopelessness over false hope or defensive hope. I know that may sound strange. Why would anyone choose the negative over the positive? But it is true. I say that because hopelessness has a value. Hopelessness in what is not real helps lead us to reality, and *reality always leads to God.* Reality is what is true; it is what *is*. When people say "It is what it is," I reso-nate with that. God created reality. If something is real, even if it is painful, God is there. And I have seen so many people over the years who, having been let down by their false hope and their defensive hope, finally gave up and entered into the right kind of hopelessness. That is, the hopelessness that gives up on what is not real and what is not truly from God. We need to feel hopeless about things like our self-effort, our control over the universe, and our ability to do it all on our own. We need to feel hopeless about things like hoping against hope that things will magically turn out OK, or that thinking positive is all we need:

> The king is not saved by a mighty army;
>> A warrior is not delivered by great strength.
> A horse is a false hope for victory;
>> Nor does it deliver anyone by its great strength.
> —Psalm 33:16–17 (NASB)

This sort of hopelessness helps us clean the slate and look for the One who provides real and substantive hope.

However, as a psychologist, I have also seen a destructive sort of hopelessness that doesn't help anyone. It occurs when an individual is clinically depressed. This type of hopelessness isn't helpful because it does not respond to any sort of hope, real or false. It can't relate to the positive. It shuts the person off from help, support, God, a good anticipation, and resources. This is because the person is either so disconnected from life and love that he doesn't have the wherewithal to reach out for hope or because he doesn't trust in hope, not wanting to be let down and devastated again. So he is stuck with no hope and no ability to experience hope.

This destructive hopelessness must be handled by a counselor with grace and sensitivity, to help the person grow into a place where he can respond to hope. Without going into the technicalities, the counselor must enter the person's hopeless mind empathically and enter his world without judgment or criticism. This takes some time. Then, when the connection is established, the counselor gradually infuses the person with the counselor's own real and true hopefulness. Finally, this helps the person to experience his reasons to hope on his own. This can be a breakthrough process for the person with no hope, but it must be done carefully.

## HOPE THAT WORKS

So what should you hope for in tough times? Well, I wish I could say that this book will show you how God will make your negative situation disappear instantly or in a short amount of time. It would be great to present some secrets and keys here that will guarantee financial stability, the right job, medical and emotional health, and restored relationships. In reality, those solutions do happen in some situations. I have experienced them in my own life and those of many others. And I hope this book will help you do your part to help them happen. Tough times can and do get better!

However, some situations do not go away, no matter what we do or however hard we pray. We don't get the guarantee, and it is unsettling and disturbing. But that is where we learn of a deeper sort of hope than simply that the problem will disappear. We learn to hope in God and in His character, that is, who He is inside Himself. We hope in the love that moves Him to be for us and in His power that strengthens us and changes our circumstances. Hope in God is never about simply finding some way to get Him to make things better, though I always pray that for myself and those I love. God has a much larger view of our lives from His vantage point. It is a view of what we need that is based on His intimate knowledge of us.

He loves you and wants to help you, but He will do it His way and in His time. God's best for you can mean a lot of things. The payoff may be today, or it may be at another time through another avenue you haven't thought of but that He provides. It may be that He creates a life full of meaning and purpose for you. It may be something He is doing internally in your soul and character. Or it may be something that you won't find out about on this side of the grave. Hope in God always, ultimately, needs to be the assured hope that *God's love will move Him to do what is best for you.*

You may think that this description of hope is too broad: *What if what is best for me is something I am afraid of? What if it's that I won't get the job that I need? Or that the marriage won't last? Or my surgery won't be successful? Can't God get more specific than that so I can feel some hope?* That concern is understandable. We all have our needs, fears, desires, and dreams that we feel strongly about, and they aren't insignificant. They need to be paid attention to. There are several sources of hope than can stand you in good stead during your struggle.

## THE PROMISES OF GOD

The Bible is full of promises from God to His people. One of their purposes is to provide real and sustaining hope for us during our darkness. God's character is reflected in His promises to us. They are commitments He makes to us so that we will know He is actively working for our best: "'For I know the plans I have for you,' says the LORD. 'They are plans for good and not for disaster, to give you a future and a hope'" (Jer. 29:11 NLT).

## NARRATIVES IN THE BIBLE

We see over and over again stories of people's lives in which God helps, rescues, changes, and transforms them. These are the underdog stories, the ones we can identify with when we are in hard times. The little guy wins: The nation of Israel is set free from slavery. David defeats Goliath. Jesus heals the demoniac. The stories give us hooks to hold on to. We see that God is active and reaching down to help His people whom He loves. He isn't sitting on His throne, waiting for the universe to wind down. He is engaged.

When I am in a difficult situation, I sometimes go to whatever I am reading in my Bible that day and ask God, "Please give me a promise or a story that will give me hope. I need it today." And time and time again, it happens.

## STORIES FROM YESTERDAY AND TODAY

I am a big believer in stories of hope from people today and in history as well. In terms of today, when the media takes the slant of "If it bleeds, it leads," we need some good news that is also true news. Real-life examples of people whose lives God has stepped into and done good things in can bring a great deal of hope. They help give us a reality check by bringing God, hard times, and our situations up close and personal. In these stories, we find people with whom we can identify because they have been there, just where we are.

There is a famous psychological experiment that measured the ability of rats to keep afloat in a fish tank full of water. There were two tanks with several rats in each. In one tank the scientists measured how long it took for rats to give up and start sinking. In the other, a scientist, at frequent intervals, reached her hand in the tank and rescued one or another of the rats from sinking. The other paddling rats observed their companions being rescued. But in the first tank, no one saw any rescue. The result of the experiment was that the rats left in the rescue tank lasted longer than those in the other. They had real hope. Seeing their buddies get help gave them more power to continue. And when we see and hear stories of people who have struggled and whom God has helped, we can tread water longer. And instead of sinking, we can swim.

## SPECIFIC PROMISES FROM GOD

I believe God specifically conveys promises of hope to people at particular times, which are for our hope. While we need to validate them through the doctrines of Scripture and through the wisdom of good people, these specific assurances can help us persevere in hardship. I have a friend who was in a bad financial fix with her adult daughter. Her daughter was a single mom, and, through financial hardship, lost her car. She couldn't get to work. My friend didn't have the means to get her daughter a car. She was worried about her daughter and her grandkids. She was praying about this situation and heard a voice say, "Candace is going to give your daughter a car." And within twenty-four hours, her friend Candace had called to offer her daughter a car. Now, my friend is not prone to wild thinking. She is a very down-to-earth businesswoman. But she heard a voice. I pressed her on this and asked, "You mean a voice like you are thinking something in your head and it seems like someone's voice?" She said, "No, I mean a voice outside my head but with nobody in the room." That event gave her hope and, in fact, gave hope to all she told about it, including myself.

# HEAVEN CAN WAIT SOMETIMES

There is a type of hopeful thinking that, in the service of heaven, negates the good things of today. These teachings are meant to provide hope in the future, but they are out of balance. The thinking is that life is terrible here, so we may as well suffer through it because heaven will be great and worth all the pain or that we should just be miserable and tolerate all the trouble and hang on for the sweet by and by. I think that is a really inferior way to get through a lifetime and one that the Bible doesn't support. Certainly heaven will be incredible. It will be a place where everything is restored, and there will be no more hard times, pain, or suffering. More than that, it is where our ultimate home is, for this world is not our home: "But our citizenship is in heaven. And we eagerly await a Savior from there, the Lord Jesus Christ" (Phil. 3:20 NIV). We are citizens of a future place we can hardly dream of. And certainly it will be much greater in quality than life here on earth. Today's life does not compare.

But that doesn't mean we should have no expectations or desire for a great life here. That is just crazy thinking and, psychologically, it contributes to a passive and disconnected experience in life. Instead, you can truly have a life very much worth living. Your years here on the planet can be full of good things. Things such as an intimate relationship with God, deep and sustaining relationships with safe people, a mission and vision that is fulfilling for you and contributes to God's purposes for the world, and a life that is satisfying, rich, and full: "The thief comes only to steal and kill and destroy; I came that they may have life, and have it abundantly" (John 10:10 NASB).

Obviously, this doesn't mean that a great life is a pain-free life. It is a life in which the pain is intertwined with joy and good things but not overwhelmed by them. It is a life that is not defined by the struggles you experience but one that makes sense of the struggles and goes beyond them into your relationships, your mission, and your purpose. You were not destined to have your struggle as your identity.

You probably have been through the exercise of figuring out what you want etched on your gravestone. It can be a helpful way to find perspective on your purpose in life. What you don't want it to say is that your struggle controlled your very life, that it formed your entire identity and the meaning of your existence: "She was very ill." "He was laid off." "She never got married." "They were in a bad car accident." You want that stone to have different words: "He loved his family." "She was a great leader." "He followed God's ways." "She made a difference." Please don't misunderstand these thoughts. I am not at all making light of difficult times; they can be devastating. Your situation may be terribly desperate or terribly sad. And you need a great deal of help, support, comfort, and resources to get through this. However, you were intended to be defined by who God made you to be and where you went with that, not by the hardships you'll face.

# CHAPTER 7

# THE GOD WHO SUFFERS WITH ME

et's look at an emotional picture of the question, "Where is God?"
What do you think of when you imagine saying that, on an
emotional level? My mind goes to a scene I have seen in several
movies, in which a grieving individual is kneeling beside the body of
someone he loved who has just died. It could be his wife, his child, or
his parents. Looking up at the sky, he screams out in sadness and pain.
The camera swings up above the scene, and as it moves higher, the two
figures become smaller and smaller until they are just a pinpoint on
the screen. It is a powerful technique. The intent of the director is to
evoke the sense of distance, aloneness, helplessness, and abandonment
that we feel when we hurt or are dealing with a difficult problem. The
director knows this is a common human experience, and he wants the
viewer to identify with that experience emotionally.

We often feel this emotion toward God in bad times. We feel as
if we are all alone with a backbreaking burden, and He is nowhere to
be found. We are the ones kneeling on the ground beside a troubled

relationship, a terrible illness, or a severe financial issue, just looking up at the sky and wondering what He is up to. During this time, even though your five senses say you are alone and He is otherwise occupied, the reality is that He is very much with you on a real and intimate level. He is suffering, feeling your distress and pain. He is not hiding behind philosophical statements or pat answers. He is deeply connected to you and your experience. He makes Himself part of your pain. And understanding the ways God suffers for you can help you a great deal in your situation.

## HAVING COMPASSION

Here is a human example of what I mean by this. When Benny was around ten years old, he needed a root canal for a bad tooth. This was a big deal at his age. Barbi brought him to the dentist, and it was simply an ordeal. Because of his age, Benny could not have a lot of anesthetic—it was too risky. So he had to feel more pain than would be normal for an adult. Barbi sat next to him as the dentist worked on the root canal. Benny tried to be brave, but the pain was excruciating. She held his arms down on the seat so he wouldn't flail at the dentist, and she saw tears trickle from his eyes down the sides of his face as the work went on. She cried along with him, knowing how much he was hurting. After a very long time, the procedure was done successfully. Even now, Benny still talks about what a nightmare it was.

Though it was certainly Benny's nightmare, it was Barbi's as well. She felt our son's pain empathetically. It was awful seeing how much he hurt and how little he understood what he was experiencing. She wanted to stop the procedure and stop the pain. She hated what he was going through. And yet she restrained herself from calling a halt to it all. Barbi knew that Benny had to go through this. She allowed it to continue. But she was not detached, cool, or professional about it.

Did that make a difference to Benny? I asked him that question as I was writing this book. I said, "You knew the pain wasn't going to stop with Mom there. What difference did that make?" He said, "I knew she was there to be there with me, and she would be there in the end." In other words, Mom's presence helped. She was present and focused on him. The pain was still the pain. It was Benny's pain, and he was the one feeling it. But he was better able to endure the situation because of his mother's compassion.

Psychologists understand that having warm and supportive relationships helps people endure bad times. They know how valuable it is for the suffering person to *be with* others when they experience all sorts of pain, from depression to loss to childhood issues. Psychologists cannot remove the difficulty or the painful feelings surrounding them, but being with a person who is struggling can make a huge difference for them. People resolve depressions, anxieties, and even medical problems sooner when they are with individuals who are compassionate and share in the feelings the person is experiencing.

The reason for this is simply that *connecting with others during difficult times makes the trials more bearable.* Relationship and connection are the delivery systems for grace, care, compassion, understanding, and a host of other good gifts. When these concepts enter our hearts and minds and become reality to us, we come more alive and are able to endure our hurts.

I don't think that relationships numb pain the way an anesthetic would. Rather, they strengthen us and support us to be better able to tolerate and endure trials well. In other words, I don't think the pain index goes down; I think the toleration index increases.

It's a little like weight training. The first time you bench press your max weight, it assaults your chest and arm muscles. But as you keep working at it, you can lift the same weight, and even more, with less stress to your body. In this analogy, your trial is the weight and the pain of the exercise. Being in relationship is the training. And your increased capacity to tolerate the burden is the result of the connections you experience.

As a leadership coach, one thing I work on with executives is their capacity to receive care and compassion from the safe people in their lives. We are in an answers- and results-based culture, and leaders are part of that. They need action steps and strategies in order to achieve results and outcomes. That is necessary and very helpful in business, finance, and work. But in the more relational parts of life, we also need to allow others to give us their empathy, and we need to accept it. The action step in that situation is to sit there, be vulnerable, and let someone in.

This is not intuitive or natural for a lot of leaders. It's outside of their training, experience base, and comfort zone. They gravitate toward wanting a measurable task to complete. In therapy sessions, I often have to say, "Talk about the hardship you are in now. I will tell you what I'm feeling for you when you do. I'll give you no advice or homework. I will simply tell you how your struggle brings me closer to you, how sad I know you are, or what a difficult thing this must be." They often reply, "I don't think this will help." But we'll go into the dialogue, and most of the time, within a few minutes, the person says something like, "Hmmm, I feel lighter (or better or more hopeful)." They are simply experiencing the physics of relationship. A burden shared is a lighter one.

Conversely, I can't think of anything worse than suffering through dark days alone. No one to "get it." No one to listen to me. And especially, no one to feel what I feel. We all have been through times like that, and the pain is much harder to bear because we are disconnected from the source of life, which is relationship. Look at it this way: Would you rather have a pain-free life but be utterly isolated? Or do you want a life with hardship but connected to those who love you? It's not really a fair question, and I am not trying to minimize the severity of your situation at all. But it helps give perspective on what is most important to you.

What is true in the relational world between humans is also true in the spiritual world with God. We benefit from experiencing the comfort of others, and we benefit from knowing His comfort as well. This is the first activity God is involved in when we have difficulties in life. In the same way that Barbi hurt alongside Benny, God hurts with you when you hurt. You are not alone in your suffering. God is in pain for you as well. When your spouse withdraws and can't be reached, God feels for you. When you fear you won't be able to take care of your family, He understands your anxiety. When you get bad news from the doctor, He shares your feeling of disorientation. This is the empathy of God. He reaches inside you and feels compassion for what you are experiencing. He has been empathizing with his people's suffering for a long time:

> Sing for joy, O heavens!
> Rejoice, O earth!
> Burst into song, O mountains!
> For the LORD has comforted his people
> and will have compassion on them in their suffering (Isa. 49:13 NLT).

> I will strengthen Judah and save Israel;
> I will restore them because of my compassion (Zech. 10:6 NLT).

> When [Jesus] saw the crowds, he had compassion on them because they were confused and helpless, like sheep without a shepherd (Matt. 9:36 NLT).

# IDENTIFYING

One of the difficulties of getting to Antarctica is four days of seasickness: two days down and two days up. Between South America and

Antarctica is the Drake Passage, where the Pacific and Atlantic Oceans meet. They are the roughest seas in the world—about five hundred miles of ten- to fifteen-foot waves. The captain told us ahead of time how it would be. He said, "Get the pills from the ship's physician and just lie down." I have decent sea legs, but when I heard the statistics, I immediately stood in line for my meds. I am glad I did. They are the only way I could have eaten for two days, with the stomach-flipping waves so strong that plates, silverware, and chairs were falling over in the dining areas the whole time. Even with the pills, it was no fun as I was somewhat queasy the whole four days. And when my stomach was stable, I was drowsy. But that was simply the price of the course. It was expected, and that is how we got to the continent.

The four days of seasickness did have a good result, however. It drew us passengers together in a way. Seeing each other green in the face, walking down the halls, holding onto the rails so we wouldn't fall, or asking, "Where is David? Haven't seen him for a couple of meals" helped us have some sense of commonality with each other. We identified with each other's discomfort. Everyone knew what everyone else was feeling. Our misery loved the company.

In the same way, God goes another step in how He suffers with you in difficulty. He not only empathizes, but He also identifies. That is, *God feels what is happening to you as if it is happening to Him.* He is not only on the outside, being with you (which is helpful in itself), but He is also on the inside, suffering as you suffer. Not just *for* you, but *with* you. On a human and psychological level, identification is why support groups are so popular and so helpful. Groups of people who have experienced the same specific troubles—lost jobs, abusive spouses, poor health, or rebellious children—do a great deal of good. Identification helps people feel normal and understood on a real-time level.

This is why it is so important that we understand Jesus' life and suffering. It is where the fullness, the completeness of the identification of

God takes place. It is difficult to imagine the majestic and omnipotent God the Father identifying with our losses, abuse, hurts, and wounds. We can see Him caring and helping, but it is a stretch to see Him being as hurt as we have been. The Incarnation of Jesus, however, transforms and clarifies all this for us. God became man and humbled Himself to feel and experience the limitations and pains of being human. He lived with us and suffered ordinary life with us: "For we do not have a high priest who is unable to sympathize with our weaknesses, but we have one who has been tempted in every way, just as we are—yet was without sin" (Heb. 4:15 NIV). He has *been there* with us.

However, Jesus moved beyond living as we live, walking as we walk, struggling as we struggle. He died for our sake, taking on all of the sins of humanity for all time, once and for all. There is no real way to fathom this experience. There are no words to describe Jesus' suffering for us. For that period on the cross, He bore the pain and penalty of all sin: "He made Him who knew no sin to be sin on our behalf, so that we might become the righteousness of God in Him" (2 Cor. 5:21 NASB).

It is also a great comfort to us that Jesus didn't suffer in silence or with a smile. He models how to withstand hard times the right way. He was emotional and verbal about what He was going through, even though He was fully and wholeheartedly committed to His plan and purpose: "While Jesus was here on earth, he offered prayers and pleadings, with a loud cry and tears, to the one who could rescue him from death" (Heb. 5:7 NLT). Sometimes people feel they are letting God down if they let it be known they hurt. Sometimes they feel they have to keep all their friends pepped up by looking at the bright side of things. It can be tiring, and it can actually work against someone beginning to feel better. How can you be comforted when you are acting happy all the time? It's much better to be emotionally honest about how we are doing. Then we are able to be comforted and start to feel better.

More to the point, however, what the suffering of God means for you and me is that the universe now has hope for being redeemed and that we have a new life. And in terms of the where-is-God question, it means He feels hurt when you feel hurt, right alongside of you. He feels the abandonment when someone leaves you for another. He experiences the weakness and devastation of your illness, the heartbreak of your wayward child, the disorientation of your economic disaster, and the horror of your abuse. There is power, help, and hope in a God who not only empathizes but also identifies with us in tough times.

I had a patient who had suffered terribly from an abusive family life as a child. He was a successful professional but had great problems in relationships and experienced depression as a result of his past. He did a great deal of hard work in therapy, faced his past, healed from it, and, over time, was quite successful in becoming a different and better person. One of the keys to all this, he told me, was thinking that when he was on the floor being beaten by an alcoholic dad, Jesus was on that floor being beaten with him. It was not a pretty picture at all; it was a picture of evil. But my patient didn't have a choice to look at a rosy past. He did not have a wonderful childhood, nor will he ever. What's happened has happened. His only choices are to see it as being in a bad place without God or with Him. It helped him in so many ways— to not feel alone; to see Jesus as hurting with him; to experience Him as not the author of his trauma but One who wanted to share in his suffering; and to face, heal, forgive, and move past what happened.

Move toward the God who suffers with you. His compassion and His identification with you will make the unbearable things bearable. But it's not always easy to make the idea of God's suffering a reality. For it to hit home for you, it must travel from head knowledge to heart understanding. I would suggest that you imagine God relating to your issue in the same way Barbi supported Benny during his root canal. He sits there next to you in the dentist chair and stays emotionally connected to you in His compassion and comfort. He does not detach Himself and say, "Just look at the bright side," or "Ignore it and keep pushing." He is weeping with those who weep and mourning with those who mourn.

Truthfully, God knows He could instantly stop your suffering if He chose to. He could miraculously restore the relationship, heal your body, or send you a lottery ticket. Sometimes He even does that, but that isn't the norm. So here He is at your side, holding the tension within Himself, seeing you hurt, looking at your eyes as you struggle to make sense of it, and restraining Himself from making it all go away for you. What is more, sometimes He holds your arms down on the armrests so you can't thrash around. That is involvement. It is "being with," in every sense of the term. It is the opposite of cool detachment and intellectual distance.

This sort of imagining is what I do personally in my tough times. I will read Bible passages that talk about God's comfort and compassion. And I will think about God as being very physically present with me, though I can't see Him. This has always helped restore my own hope so that I can continue down the path of life He has for me. Trust in and value the benefit of God's compassion and identification.

# CHAPTER 8

# THE GOD WHO WORKS BEHIND THE SCENES

D uring difficult times, you need to know and experience the presence and comfort of God. You need to believe that He is with you *in the moment*. However, that is not enough. You also need to know that He is not only connecting with you at a deep level, but He is acting for you, in you, and with you. He is not passive or resigned to your situation, nor should you be. He is *doing* as much as He is *being* in your circumstance. I would not feel a lot of trust or hope in God if He was simply in touch with me without any impetus, power, or force to accomplish things. I would be afraid that I was living in a universe that was randomly spinning out of control. I would fear God had no thought for my safety or welfare or for that of those I love. In the same way a child needs to know that her parents are looking out for her even when they are not nearby, you need to know that God is using His power to produce good things in your life even when you can't see Him. You may not always know the end game, but He is working for you.

To illustrate this, I have been involved for years in the design of the Web sites that I use in my work. They have lots of different uses, such as providing information, video content, ideas, resources, and services. I love the power and creativity of Web design though I am not on the technical end of things. I am always amazed at the webmasters I work with. Because the Internet morphs so quickly, with new ways of communicating becoming instantly viral, Web experts are always changing their strategies in a very fluid way. I will talk to a webmaster about a design need, perhaps to make a resource more prominent or simplify the way we access some information or insert a new service. And then the next day or so, I'll get online and, like magic, the site reflects that conversation. A new section or tab or photo appears. Like the Wizard of Oz, I never see the webmaster doing his work. In fact, sometimes I never even meet him or her face-to-face, only by phone and e-mail. But the behind-the-scenes movement is going on, whether or not it is apparent to me how it happens.

In the same way, God is working behind the scenes in our lives in ways we can't see, to bring a better good to us. Though He allows us to have tough days, He does not allow them to defeat His purposes and goals for us. He will win in the end, and He is winning now, even though times can be dark. Not only that, but He is bringing those who love Him into the ultimate victory: "And we know that God causes everything to work together for the good of those who love God and are called according to his purpose for them" (Rom. 8:28 NLT).

## BILL'S STORY

A good friend of mine, Bill Dallas, is an example of this principle. He was convicted of financial crimes and incarcerated in the prison at San Quentin. Though he knew he was guilty, he had expected to serve his time in a facility for white collar, nonviolent criminals. He did not come from an impoverished background, he was a student leader in high school, and he graduated from Vanderbilt University. So to live in San Quentin, alongside murderers and rapists serving long sentences, was a major shock. Bill was devastated and could not adjust. Within a short period of time, he became depressed and suicidal in prison. He had no hope; he did not want to survive. But a couple of inmates befriended him and began to support him. Finally, they helped him get a job at the prison television station, a position for which he had no experience.

During this time, Bill was in the midst of deep spiritual growth. And when he was released, he had a vision of what he believed God was calling him to. He started working in the Christian media industry, eventually founding a company called Church Communication Network. The company provides many kinds of avenues for Christian media, from producing television show content on a satellite network to creating live simulcast speaking events. I partner with CCN to produce my content and talks. They are a major force in getting spiritual content to people and churches on a worldwide level.

Let's unpack Bill's path in terms of the subject of God and hard times. God was actively working on Bill's behalf in His unseen fashion. Look at the events: An unusual prison setting that broke Bill. Unlikely men who helped restore him. A job working for a television station. As the old saying goes, God was closing doors and opening new ones. Bill would never have dreamed his life would have ended up like it has, but he believes God's hand has been on him.[1]

It's important to also notice that Bill's situation was largely his fault, as he will readily admit. He was not the victim of a tornado, nor did he contract a chronic disease, nor did he lose his life savings in a corrupted stock market. Bill put himself in his difficulty. This is important because we are often less likely to look for God's work when we have dug our own hole. We usually think, *I got myself into this mess; I'll have to get myself out.* But the mess he was in was far too over-whelming for him to rescue himself through self-effort or willpower. So, as most of this book concerns difficulties that may largely not be your fault, Bill's story should encourage you to look to, love, and trust the hand of God even when your sin has caused your heartache. If He is looking so closely after someone who has blown up his own life, He is certainly doing the same for someone who has suffered a blow that wasn't of his own doing.

I love the story of Elisha's servant. It is one of my favorite illus-trations of God's unseen activity, and it's good for us to remember in difficult times. In the story, Elisha, the prophet, had been advising the king of Israel on military matters, as Israel was in conflict with the nation of Aram (Syria). Elisha's advice was sound, and Israel was suc-cessful against her enemies. So the king of Aram planned to neutralize Elisha, the asset, and brings lots of military firepower to capture him. Elisha's servant sees the attackers and is terrified:

> When the servant of the man of God got up early the next morning and went outside, there were troops, horses, and chariots everywhere. "Oh, sir, what will we do now?" the young man cried to Elisha.
>
> "Don't be afraid!" Elisha told him. "For there are more on our side than on theirs!" Then Elisha prayed, "O LORD, open his eyes and let him see!" The LORD opened the young man's eyes, and when he looked up, he saw that the hillside around Elisha was filled with horses and chariots of fire.
>
> As the Aramean army advanced toward him, Elisha prayed, "O LORD, please make them blind." So the LORD struck them with blindness as Elisha had asked.
> —2 Kings 6:15–18 (NLT)

Elisha was aware of what his servant was not able to see. The prophet knew there was another reality, one that was actually more substantive and powerful than the army standing around them. Until his eyes were opened, the young man could see only the present-day reality. No wonder the servant was afraid. He could see only the dangers, and they were great.

This story can help you to realize that there are good things going on behind the scenes when you are in dark days. God is present, active, and protective. It also illustrates that you don't have to pretend that your circumstances aren't hard. Psychologically speaking, it isn't a sign of great faith that you go into denial or minimize or rationalize your circumstances. An attacking army is a scary thing. So is a job loss or a health hardship. Our hope doesn't come from acting as though the hardship doesn't exist. It comes, rather, from understanding that there are greater forces around us than that hardship.

Here is the principle: *Reality has nothing to do with what is visible or invisible. It has everything to do with God.* God is the author of both the seen and the unseen worlds, and only He can see both. Sometimes the unseen is more powerful than the seen. This is not easy to learn. It has a lot to do with faith, which we will deal with in a few chapters. But it is good to ask God to give you eyes to see His horses and chariots of fire when you are struggling.

## THE PLAN OVER TIME

There are those events in which we see God's work instantly, as in the Elisha story. However, my experience is that most of the time this is not the case. Most of the time, it takes time. God works things out over a sequence of events, and sometimes we find out much later what He was up to. For example, years ago, Dr. Henry Cloud and I partnered with Drs. Frank Minirth, Paul Meier, and Dave Stoop to create a mental health treatment system. We designed and operated the system for ten years. It was one of the most fulfilling times of my life up to that point. I was involved in helping people resolve depressions, anxiety disorders, substance abuse, and a number of other debilitating emotional issues. Additionally, the psychological principles of the program were based on biblical constructs. So I was part of an organization that was using the Bible to do permanent healing for people. The system was researched and shown to have significant results over a lengthy period of time. I could not imagine a better work life. It was, as far as I was concerned, the intersection of my passion and my mission.

Then the health insurance industry began making changes in how it reimbursed medical care. This was a major shift in both the insurance and medical sectors. It was complicated, as it involved care issues, responsibility problems in both medicine and in insurance structures, and economics. But the upshot of it was that it reduced the length of a mental health patient's hospital stay dramatically. Normally patients were able to stay in treatment for a few weeks, but now it was a few days. The problem was, in the model we developed, longer stays were necessary and critical because they allowed the patients to attend and participate in the intensive therapy groups several times a day over a long period of time. That sort of longevity helped them to experience the culture of the unit, feel safe, be accepted and connected, and open up their hearts to others there. They were able to make full use of the therapists and mental health workers. That openness was a very significant component of the treatment, as the doctors, therapists, and group members could be part of the deep healing and restoration that was necessary to resolve the issues underlying the depressions and anxiety.

It takes more than a couple of days to feel safe enough to open up to others. A few days didn't allow our psychological model to work. The organization was no longer viable, so we sold it. I remember wondering what in the world God was doing. After seeing so many people do so well for so long, at such a deep level, I couldn't make sense of it. Why would a good thing go away? I didn't really understand it on a big picture level.

Time passed. A few months after we sold our practice, something began changing in my work life. Other opportunities began to arise. I began to find new avenues of delivery for the model of spiritual and emotional growth that had been researched and developed in the hospital programs. I began finding new ways to write and speak to people who didn't need to be hospitalized but just wanted better lives and relationships. I began using the model to write about relationships, dating, marriage, parenting, business, leadership, and a host of other topics. Media opportunities began developing. I began to consult with organizations using the model in a way that fit their own contexts and issues. And what I noticed was a lot of other people were being helped in much broader areas of life.

I don't know the whole story here or exactly what God was doing behind the scenes. Most likely, I would not have had the time, space, or energy to continue operating the health care system at that level *and* do what I am doing now. I now know, in ways I had never dreamed of, that my own mission in life has been carried further since those hospital days. Where was God? He was constructing a new reality for me—one in which good things happened. And I didn't get the instant photo; I got the video version over time.

In the book of Genesis, the story of Joseph, son of Jacob, is a much more extreme example of seeing God work over time. Joseph suffered greatly for years. Look at the events he experienced: He was thrown in a pit by his brothers and sold as a slave. At age seventeen, he was framed for attempted rape and imprisoned until he was thirty. A prisoner whom he helped and befriended forgot him. This is someone who could legitimately say, "Where is God?" Yet at the end of the story, when he talks to his brothers about their cruelty, he says, "You intended to harm me, but God intended it all for good. He brought me to this position so I could save the lives of many people" (Gen. 50:20 NLT). The "many people" are the Egyptians and his own family. Joseph's leadership helped a huge number of individuals to survive years of devastating famine. There is no way that Joseph could have foreseen God working behind the scenes at the time of his suffering. But in the end, over time, Joseph understood the bigger picture.

## KEEPING BOTH REALITIES IN PLACE

Even though this is a helpful and important reality, I think this may be one of the hardest things to understand about where God is in our tough times. When you lose your job in a hard economy or your marriage falls apart, you just want to get your life back: a new job, a restored marriage. There tends to be little interest in what's behind this. By nature, we are not a people who easily look beyond our circumstances to the deeper meaning. In fact, to be perfectly honest, we often don't care what the *lesson* or *purpose* is behind the scenes. As I mentioned before, most of the time we just want the trouble to end so we can go back to life.

This is especially true if the difficulty lies in something that is reasonable, good, and normal, such as a decent job, a good marriage, or personal health. *I'm not asking for all that much in the first place* is foremost in our minds. It's not as if we are asking to be picked for the top spot in the company or to have all the money in the world. This sense of reasonable requests makes it harder to look beyond the trials to see God's hand in it all. Yet if we can look further than the situation, it can be enormously helpful to see what God may be doing.

This doesn't mean we should deny or dismiss our experiences or our feelings about our situations. Remember again that God never denies your pain. The task is to actually experience where we are in the present while being aware of other realities that are going on at the same time. We are to be attuned both to what's going on and also to what's behind what's going on. I know this may sound a little schizophrenic, but it is not. It is healthy adult functioning. We do it all the time. The last time you watched a good movie, you probably did it. You got emotionally involved in the plot and characters and cared about what was going on in the story. At the same time, you noticed the mood the director was setting up, you started to guess a plot twist, or you were aware of a weakness or some lapse in credibility in the movie. You were there in the film, and you were looking beyond the film.

This ability is one of the traits of maturity. Children don't come packaged with it. For them, the present is all that matters. There is no other reality that they care about. Our kids have never said, "Thanks for the broccoli. I know it doesn't taste as good as pizza, but the nutrients are more wholesome." (I'm sure some kids have said that, but not ours!) That ability to see other factors comes with time and has to be developed. This is simply true for us in life, in love, in career, and in understanding hard times.

## GETTING DOWN TO WHAT IS REALLY IMPORTANT

There is another phenomenon I have noticed, and that is how people are getting down to core values in hard times. This is an indication that God is working behind the scenes in our difficulties. For example, I talked to a neighbor of mine recently who is a corporate executive. He could be on the verge of losing his position within his company, and he is a family man with a mortgage, like so many others in his situation. I asked him how he was doing. He said, "Well, I've been in the business world awhile, so I've weathered this before. It's not fun. But at the same time, it is helping me to look at what I really want to do in life and expanding how I'm looking at my interests and opportunities." My neighbor is looking to see what is behind his situation, though it hasn't become clear yet. But I know him, and I know he will use his circumstances to do what he was telling me.

During this economic downturn, I have heard story after story like this, especially in the area of careers. It is as if the current situation is giving people the opportunity to think, *Who am I, what am I about, and where does God want me?* The loss of job security becomes a time to rethink life, passion, interest, and spiritual values. It happens in a way that would have been less likely if the job had remained the same. God comes front and center, where He belongs in our lives and in the universe. We see His activity; we know He is working for our good and for His purposes: "But as for me, God will redeem my life. He will snatch me from the power of the grave" (Ps. 49:15 NLT).

# CHAPTER 9

# THE GOD WHO TRANSFORMS YOU

I was talking to a friend of mine about making an appointment to take my car in for a scheduled maintenance visit. He told me his approach to this tradition, and it was one of the strangest yet most illuminating things I have ever heard. He said, "Whenever I take my car in, I tell them to find something."

Confused, I said, "Find something?"

He said, "Yes, I tell them to find something wrong. I want them to look so hard that they find something to fix. I don't want them to lie about it. But what I really, really don't want is to have my car break down at 3:00 a.m. on the highway. So I just tell them to find something."

Though I have not adopted my friend's practice, it illustrates something very important that God does in your difficult times. Just as the mechanic is investigating, analyzing, stress testing, and diagnosing your car, God uses hard days to do the same with you. He uses your struggles to help you in the areas of growth you need to be helped on, and over time, He makes you into a new and different person. This process of growth and change is called *transformation*. It refers to God's design for you to become, from the inside out, someone who is more mature, more developed, and more like Christ: "And we, who with unveiled faces all reflect the Lord's glory, are being transformed into his likeness with ever-increasing glory, which comes from the Lord, who is the Spirit" (2 Cor. 3:18 NIV). Growth is one of the most important and helpful things you can be engaged in, in all of life. So, like my friend does with his car, it is a good strategy to approach your own tough times by saying to God, "Find something," and seeing what happens. His design is to create you into someone better than you dreamed you could be—a new person who is different and improved from the inside out.

## NOT YET WHO WE NEED TO BE

All of us need help to grow and change in our hearts, minds, and behavior. We are an unfinished people. We are not yet who we need to be. As the saying goes, whoever thinks they have it all together is someone you probably need to keep your eye on. We find ourselves failing in some responsibility, having a habit we can't break or allowing toxic relationships to control us when we know they aren't good for us. The growth process was designed by God to change us into people who can live life at a higher level of functioning and are more competent in what life revolves around. And that process is moved along by difficult circumstances.

This idea is simply a law of the universe. You don't have to even believe in a higher being to see that difficult circumstances can help transform us into a far better people than we are. Look at the overcomers who inspire us with the things they have achieved in the face of struggle: Helen Keller. Steven Hawking. Abraham Lincoln. We see them manage tremendous burdens to become people who accomplish greatness through their perseverance. Likewise, look at successful athletes who endure a different kind of discomfort—the pain of intensive training at unbelievable levels to achieve world-class competence. I have never met anyone whom I consider to have reached his or her full potential, who has not overcome significant difficult circumstances to get to where they are now. Struggle is not the only ingredient for growth, but it is a necessary one. The Bible affirms that God uses hard times to make us better, even going so far as to teach us to be happy about our circumstances:

> We can rejoice, too, when we run into problems and trials, for we know that they help us develop endurance. And endurance develops strength of character, and character strengthens our confident hope of salvation. And this hope will not lead to disappointment. For we know how dearly God loves us, because he has given us the Holy Spirit to fill our hearts with his love.
> —Romans 5:3–5 (NLT)

This is certainly counterintuitive. The word *rejoice* seems impossible to experience when we are in difficult times. I don't feel happy when I am struggling. Much of the time, I hate it. However, the verse doesn't say that we must feel happy when we hurt. The Greek word is not as much a term of emotion as it is a term of attitude and value. It literally means "boast." Rather than simply feeling happy, it is a stance, an attitude. It is experiencing and understanding a matter as positive in its nature or outcome. You may lift up the fact that you're going to the dentist because you'll get rid of your toothache. You may exalt the reality that you are going to the gym because you'll get in shape. In the same way, you may rejoice that you are having a financial or health problem because you know that personal growth will come out of it somehow. For many of us, the mantra is "avoid pain at all costs." But the reality is that pain can be a character builder if we allow it to work that way.

However, I never like it when people say to those who are suffering, "This will build your character." That may be the worst bedside manner possible and the worst timing possible. It can devalue the pain of the person. It can make them feel guilty because they're not cheering for their own growth. It can make them feel disconnected from others, thinking, *My life is upside down, and this isn't helping.* It even has a condescending parental tone to it: "I know you're in time-out right now, but this will be good for you."

There is a sequence to this: Empathy first. Perspective second. People just need to know they are heard where they are in their experiences before they can listen to advice or insight. I often coach individuals who are supporting someone in hard times, and I suggest that they ask permission before sharing their opinions: "Would you be open to my perspective on your situation?" A more reflective struggler may think that in the first place: *What am I learning about myself from all this?* All that being said, however it happens, the growth aspect of hard times is a very valuable benefit, as we will see.

This may not be you. You may not be very interested in how God is changing you during hard times. That may not be something you value or something on your personal radar screen. I know lots of people who have little interest in growth or transformation. Most of these people are good folks, but self-improvement or wanting to engage in some sort of change process is just not an intentional part of their life agenda. They are the ones who, when I meet them and we trade career info, have absolutely nothing to say when I tell them I am a *Christian psychologist.* One of those words is foreign enough, and both together simply create a great opportunity to talk about sports! However, Christians can also be uninvolved in the growth process. We all understand the idea of someone attending church and living a moral and good life with no deeper involvement in matters of change.

Interest or no interest, however, God is working with you and on you! He wants you to change and improve in some important ways, and those ways are for your good. That is how He designed us all: "Instead, we will speak the truth in love, growing in every way more and more like Christ, who is the head of his body, the church" (Eph. 4:15 NLT). In addition, personal growth will help you to deal with your difficulties from a more healthy and whole standpoint. In medicine, a doctor may postpone a surgery because the patient is too sick to stand it and could have a system failure or be susceptible to infections. Then when the patient receives more nutrients, rest, a strengthened autoimmune system, and so forth, the doctor is more confident that the patient will be able to successfully tolerate the surgery. The healthier you are, the more capacity you have to handle your hard times.

## DESTINY

Your growth not only will help you handle your present situation, it also will help you reach your destiny and purpose in life. Personal growth both *repairs* us and *prepares* us. Most of us can relate to the idea of wanting to reach our potential and become the person we were meant to be. We tend to think of this in terms of task, mission, job, passion, and career. For example, kids dream of being athletes or actors. As adults, we have heroes and mentors. However, destiny has a DNA to it. It has requirements underneath the purpose. In other words, you find your destiny when you become the person who best fits the destiny.

We don't come into the world in a state of readiness to live out our destiny. A baby is a squirming mass of potential. She has a life with meaning and purpose ahead of her. But it takes years and years of experiences for that infant to become a person who is living out the destiny God implanted in her, ages before she was born. God has some hat He wants you to wear: that of a businessperson, a service provider, an engineer, a professional, a teacher, a parent, or some combination of things. That is the big plan. You were meant to make a positive difference and to experience joy and satisfaction in doing it. However, in order to reach, discover, and experience that destiny, you must become the right kind of person along the way. We are designed to develop our character as a framework to help fulfill our destiny. Part of that work comes through experiencing and learning from hard times. Your present difficulty may be moving you down the path of growth that you need to experience in order to fulfill the "good works" of God. That is what growth is all about. It is a building and a transforming of your internal character. So let's understand what character is.

## CHARACTER: MEETING THE DEMANDS OF REALITY

Most of us have some sort of an idea of what *character* is. We tend to think of a person with character as someone who has a moral basis for life, integrity in his dealings with others, and is an honorable citizen. However, while those traits are a part of character, they do not make up the entire picture. A more complete way to understand character is that it is the set of abilities you need to meet life's demands. Life requires much from us. We have to maintain our relationships, take ownership of our lives, deal with finances and careers, parent kids, and so forth. These requirements are the demands of life. They aren't bad; in fact, they are very good. But we must have certain capacities and abilities in order to meet all those demands. A person with a good moral basis, integrity, and honor can be deficient in other parts of her life. For example, she may find it hard to open up and be emotionally vulnerable with people, which is just as important an ability to have. So it's helpful to take a look at the basic hallmarks of character. These capacities are the right stuff needed in order to achieve what you were intended to achieve and become what you were intended to become. Here is an overview of those abilities:

- CONNECTION: being with and trusting safe people, letting them in, and being vulnerable with them. We need to need other people. God uses people to provide the grace, fuel, love, support, and validation we all need. The person who can't let others in is in jeopardy of running out of gas and not being able to function at high levels during stressful times.
- DEFINITION: being a separate and honest person, clear on your responsibilities and boundaries in life. When we are defined, we know who we are and who we aren't. And we know the extents and limits of our responsibilities.
- REALITY: dealing successfully with the negative aspects of life, such as your own imperfections and the failures of others. When you can deal with reality, you can handle the bad times with skill and competence.
- COMPETENCE: growing into an adult who is confident of herself and her purpose in life. A competent person is able to invest her gifts and talents in ways that help the world be a better place, as well as further her own goals.

When you look at these, it is easy to see what a difference they can make in life, love, and career. They are the toolbox that equips us to solve our problems and meet our God-given goals. Henry Cloud and I have written about these aspects of character capacities in several other books.[1] These abilities are worth investing in and developing.

Development is an important part of growing character. Character can't be gained in any other way but through a process of experiences over time. We can't gain character by simply reading a book. We must have interactions with ourselves, with reality, and with others to develop it. And many of those experiences involve struggle. For example, a house foreclosure is a major crisis. It disrupts all of a person's life. It certainly qualifies as a trial. But it helps develop endurance, and from that, strength of character. It can build us up instead of disheartening us. If you refer to the Bible passage in Romans quoted earlier in this chapter, you will see the word *character*. The original Greek word actually means "experience." Again, you cannot separate character from experience. There is no shortcut.

## HOW IT WORKS

Hard times affect us all, and they simply can't be ignored. They will get our attention. When your car is stuck on the train tracks, the train speeding in your direction has your full attention. Conversely, when life is going normally or "as it should," we usually are not as intentional about our growth as we should be. Here are some examples of how character is developed through struggle.

### CONNECTION

Tough times bring us to the end of our own abilities to go it alone or to be self-sufficient. They help drive us to open up to the support and attachment of others. They basically show us our incompleteness outside of relationship. For example, a very successful business friend of mine was a very disconnected person. He was nice, had good values and principles, but had little interest in being vulnerable and letting other people know him deeply. Then his wife became very ill with a serious, chronic medical condition. He was devastated. He had never encountered a problem that he could not solve with his intelligence and discipline. This was beyond him. He could not do anything to help her condition.

Ultimately, he took the step of opening up to some men who had reached out to him. He began to talk about his fears that she would die, his sadness at what the illness was doing to her, his anxiety about their kids, and his need for her. The men were supportive and warm with him. Gradually, over time, he became more emotionally accessible, as psychologists call it. This brought him closer to his wife, his children, himself, and even to God. Eventually, his wife's condition stabilized, though she did not fully recover. They learned how to live with her condition. And he became a much more open, engaged, and vulnerable person.

## DEFINITION

God uses hard circumstances to make us more honest and clear people. We often have a tendency to go with the flow, not make waves, and not disagree with others for fear of causing conflict or making others angry with us. We become centered on people-pleasing and even what is called *enabling* others so as not to make anyone unhappy. You may be familiar with the word *codependence*. It refers to the problem of not defining ourselves clearly and instead rescuing others' bad behavior. But difficulty can help us work through the vagueness of personality and the fears of conflict to become someone who is separate from the crowd, truly aware of who they are in Christ.

A crisis sometimes brings out the truthfulness in us. A married couple who are friends of mine had these tendencies to go with the flow until their teenage son became a drug addict. Not a recreational user but an addict. He was out of control. They had tried to be loving, positive, and encouraging, and they had been afraid to set limits with him. They didn't want to alienate him or make him feel bad. But his condition became so extreme, to the point he was stealing items from their home to sell them to buy drugs, they had him arrested. This was the hardest thing they had ever done. And they tell me that it is one of the best things they have ever done. The arrest got his attention. He finally became open to treatment. Now, years later, he is still clean and sober and a husband and father. I would not wish his past on anyone, but the benefit to his parents, besides the obvious, is that they are more defined, clear, and honest people now. They do not let their fears of others' rejection muddy up their decisions and values.[2]

## DEALING WITH NEGATIVE REALITIES

Most of us have some tendencies toward perfectionism. At the very least, we wish our friends and families were perfect! We have difficulty accepting negatives and sometimes do not handle failure well. Of all the character attributes, I think hard circumstances most effectively help us grow in this particular area. Struggle simply changes our paradigm of life. It helps us move from the demand to be perfect to the capacity to be a real person. Difficult times do not allow us to live in a tower of ideals, longing for the way things *should be*; they move us toward embracing the way things *are*.

A friend of mine, a corporate executive, was part of the fallout from his giant company's demise. Before his business crashed, he was a very nice person, but he tended to portray an image of having everything together. He had the perfect marriage, kids, house, faith, and physique. He wasn't at all arrogant, just very together without any loose ends. His life was pretty close to ideal. Sometimes it was a little hard talking to him about my normal struggles because it seemed he had no point of reference for those experiences. He would be sympathetic, but beyond that, he really had nothing through which he could identify with me.

That all changed when his job vanished. As we would talk, he became more comfortable with negatives. In His own way, I believe that God brought some negative realities to him so he would have to deal with them. Fortunately, my friend didn't fight it or go into some state of denial. Instead, he opened up about his struggles, his own failures, even his anger at the irresponsible economic practices of his company. He talked about his own family of origin and the way it wasn't OK to have a down day or anything but victories when he was a kid. And he was able to understand my struggles on an authentic level. In fact, he is simply more relaxed and approachable now. He is still dealing with the job situation; however, he now can be more flexible, more adaptive, and more realistic about how he goes about it. That is a side benefit of the growth he has experienced from his troubles.

## INVESTING GIFTS AND TALENTS AS AN ADULT IN THE WORLD

We are designed to ultimately take our place as grown-ups in the world. There is a purpose we have, a mission, which we have been given the gifts, abilities, and passions to execute. We should be looking for a way to give back and make things better. And to do that, we need to relate to others as adults, not as children. That is, we grow up and give up our need for others to approve of everything we do, and we become people who seek the approval of God alone: "Do your best to present yourself to God as one approved, a workman who does not need to be ashamed and who correctly handles the word of truth" (2 Tim. 2:15 NIV).

Difficult life problems can also be used by God to help us develop the capacity to function as a grown-up. They move us to expand our gifts and abilities to new levels. Elena, now in her forties, lost her first husband in a terrible traffic accident in her twenties. I asked her how she made it through that. She answered, "My son."

"What do you mean?" I asked.

She said, "We had an eighteen-month-old son. I was totally devastated because my husband and my marriage were my whole life. I was pretty inconsolable and very depressed. I thought about giving up many times. And then I thought, *I have to keep going for my son.* I had to be the adult, for he had no choice but to be a child. He was totally dependent on me and needed me to be around. I loved him. But not only that, he was my duty and obligation as well. So I would get out of bed every day, take care of him, and do whatever I had to do that day."

She didn't do this on her own. She had a close family and friendship support system that helped her. But deep within her, she became a more adult person, taking on her duties as a mom, and that helped both her son and her. In fact, that ability to go her own way has carried her well through the last two decades. She formed her own business, remarried, had another child, and is active in her community. We could ask, "Would she have done these things anyway had she not been widowed?" We don't know. What we do know is that she has used her loss to become a high-functioning adult and professional person, investing herself in giving back.

So God uses hard times—when we allow Him to—to help us develop the necessary character traits to fulfill our destiny, our good works. That doesn't make our pains less difficult. But it does help us to understand and make use of them. We don't naturally gravitate toward this. We would all prefer the destiny without the work, wouldn't we? It's the difference in the way we see relationships in romantic comedy movies and real-life growth. In the movies, the couples originally meet and hate each other. She is an obsessive control freak, and he is a little boy who won't grow up. He resents her uptight nature, and she finds him irresponsible and flaky. They have a series of adventures that throw them together. At the last minute, they find that they were meant for each other and are a great fit; it's all good. There has been little character change or growth or introspection. They just experience that love conquers all.

I am a total believer in love as well, but it doesn't conquer all. Love helps make the difficult work of growth move along with grace and support. And in reality, couples who want to love more work hard at opening up, being safe for each other, telling the truth, and taking ownership of their lives. They change for each other and for the good. And then they experience their destiny of having a loving marriage. My point is that growth requires work, and becoming a transformed person requires more work. Don't fight the hardship you have. Use it and learn from it to grow and change.

## THE VERTICAL AND THE HORIZONTAL

In working with many people on these issues for a long time, I have noticed that there is sometimes a difference between certain kinds of people, especially in how they address hard times. Some seem to really have their spiritual disciplines and commitments together—they know the Bible, they pray often, and they put God first in their lives. But they don't pay attention to their personal character growth issues. These personal issues are also deeply spiritual matters as well, but more on a horizontal level than a vertical one. It is hard for these deeply spiritual people to have authentic human relationships, to be vulnerable and real with others. They are "so heavenly minded that they are no earthly good." I have seen this imbalance interfere with their abilities to find God and His help in hard times. They seek Him and ask for Him, but they tend to miss what He might want them to learn in their situations.

On the other hand, I know a lot of people who work hard on their character growth but have an undeveloped faith life. Similarly, while they do well on the horizontal, the weakness of the vertical prevents a full expression between themselves and God in what He wants to help them with and accomplish in them. That is why we need to see spiritual growth as encompassing the horizontal as well as the vertical.

Relational growth brings us closer to God; closeness to God promotes relational growth. In this way, we experience life the way we were designed to live it:

> Instead, we will speak the truth in love, growing in every way more and more like Christ, who is the head of his body, the church. He makes the whole body fit together perfectly. As each part does its own special work, it helps the other parts grow, so that the whole body is healthy and growing and full of love.
> —Ephesians 4:15–16 (NLT)

In other words, God uses our relationships so we grow closer to Him.

## HARD TIMES THAT CAUSE DAMAGE

You may be thinking at this point, *I had some hard times that did not grow me. They harmed me and injured me.* And this may be true. Not every hardship is one that, as in the above examples, drives us toward growth. Those are hard times that *direct us.* But there are also difficult circumstances that do not direct us as much as they *damage* us. No one would say they are good for you. Damage is damage. In fact, and this is very important, *often we do not possess the character maturity we need because of damage in our past.* That is, we experience, especially in significant relationships, hurtful patterns that prevent us from developing the way God intended. Our hearts basically go into hiding and stop growing in an injured state. Child abuse can do this. So can trauma or the premature loss of a loved one. Alcoholism and drugs in the family can stunt personal development. A family pattern of overcontrol, shame and guilt messages, and perfectionistic pressures all damage us. The list goes on, but the point is that there is a difference between struggles that help us grow and struggles from which we need to heal and repair. The way I have most often seen God work is that He uses our present-day financial, relational, or medical problems to show us that there are some earlier injuries in us caused by earlier hard times. The present-day stress tests unearth our lack of connection, definition, reality, or competence. And using these as guides, He helps direct us to the wholeness and transformation He designed for us. Then as our experiences change us and our minds understand healthier ways to deal with life's demands, we are transformed: "Don't copy the behavior and customs of this world, but let God transform you into a new person by changing the way you think. Then you will learn to know God's will for you, which is good and pleasing and perfect" (Rom. 12:2 NLT).

# CHAPTER 10

# THE GOD WHO CONNECTS YOU WITH OTHERS

Where do you go when hard times hit? Not physically but in your mind. Most of the time, our tendency is to enter our internal "cave." That is, when we are faced with a disaster, we naturally shut down, withdraw from it all, and try to figure things out on our own, reemerging into life when we have some sense of centeredness. Though this sounds more male than female, women aren't exempt from this pattern of behavior. While we all certainly need our cave-times in order to have some space for ourselves and gain perspective, most of us have the habit of shutting down so much that we simply don't let other people in to how we are really doing; no one enters the deeper parts of ourselves where we live with the situation that plagues us. This tendency keeps us unplugged from one of the greatest and most valuable sources of help and support that God provides: *relationship*. Relationship, connecting with others on a need level, will often make the difference between a crisis overcoming you, or you overcoming it. The encouraging reality is that *struggle itself can drive you to relationship.* Even if you are a cave-person and tend to isolate, one of God's activities in tough times is to move you, influence you, and help you make relationships that will support you both now and in the future.

The Bible describes the importance of connecting in relationship, using *light* as a metaphor. For example, "For once you were full of darkness, but now you have light from the Lord. So live as people of light" (Eph. 5:8 NLT); "For you are all children of the light and of the day; we don't belong to darkness and night" (1 Thess. 5:5 NLT). The more we expose parts of our lives to the light of connection, the less darkness and emptiness we'll experience in our souls. One of my Antarctic excursions was to camp out overnight on the mainland in a pup tent. After my partner and I set up the tent and supported it with snow walls, we went to bed in our sleeping bags. I slept a total of about forty-five minutes the entire night. It wasn't because of the cold temperature since our insulation was fine. It was the light. The Antarctic summer sun was up twenty-two out of twenty-four hours a day. So 3:00 a.m. looked like noon. The tent's material didn't keep the sunlight out, and I didn't bring an eye mask. The light kept me awake even when I didn't want to be. In the same way, the light of relationship and connecting with others is one of God's ways of waking up your own life and heart when hard times begin to shut you down.

The earliest difficult circumstance anyone experiences in life is not during marriage, parenting, the teen years, or grade school. It is at birth. While childbirth is a great and blessed event for parents, it is actually pretty traumatic for the newborn. Pushed and pulled from a warm and comfortable environment, the infant is thrust into a strange world of blinding lights, pain, and strange sounds. I was present at both of our sons' births, and I remember their faces. They weren't smiling. They were shrieking. Miserable. However, God put into place an answer for the newborn, and that answer is a mom. As a baby's life-support system, a mother makes things safe and soothes, calms, and stabilizes the child. In so doing, she is modeling that relationship is a good thing for him, whatever his need.

## THE NORM FOR ALL OF LIFE

Sometimes people worry about reaching out to humans instead of God when they hurt. They wonder if it means they are not trusting God or letting God meet their every need. They feel a little guilty, sometimes even disloyal to God. It is as if God's plan is for us to seek only Him and pray, and if we need a friend, a small group, or a therapist, we aren't spiritual enough. However, this just isn't what the Bible teaches. The message of Scripture is that God wants us to connect both with Him and also with each other.[1]

Connecting with God and people is a both-and, not an either-or, prospect. Above all, *in difficult times you need people to whom you can open up.* If there is any season of life in which you need to learn to reach out, take risks, and let people in at a deep level, it is during a crisis. When your resources are down the most and your anxiety is spiking, you need people all the more. The Bible teaches this in many places, in principles and in stories. For example, God sent Titus to Paul to comfort Paul in his own difficult circumstances: "For even when we came into Macedonia our flesh had no rest, but we were afflicted on every side: conflicts without, fears within. But God, who comforts the depressed, comforted us by the coming of Titus" (2 Cor. 7:5–6 NASB). He could have spoken in a still, small voice or sent an angel or created a miracle for Paul to be encouraged. And God does do that at times. But at other times he sends a person to help, as the phrase goes: *Jesus with skin on.* Job's friends sat with him for a week without speaking, to comfort him, "for they saw that his suffering was too great for words"

(Job 2:13 NLT). There are times that people bring comfort to us simply by their presence rather than their words.

It's important to emphasize, however, that people are not just our 911 call. They are our maintenance for support and help through life, good times and bad, ups and downs. Our need for relationship is not about keeping life together on our own until we are redlining or absolutely out of gas (another male tendency, but again, women are also guilty of it). Instead, we are to experience relationship as *the context in which life happens*. Life should be lived in relationship. It's how we experience accomplishment. Good times. Family. Love. Work. Vacations. Nothing really significant happens outside of relationship. And I have noticed that, in many cases, it takes a crisis for a person to understand the importance of relationship. In that sense, hardship is designed to launch us into a lifestyle of relationship. Permanently. So if people help you get through your present darkness, don't stop going to them when it's over. Stay in connection. It is not for just the panic button but for everyday life: "This is my command: Love each other" (John 15:17 NLT).

## THE CHANGE

I can't keep count of all the times I have seen how hard times make people much more relationally accessible than they were before their difficulty. It is simply staggering. Those who learn how to connect through their hurts really do change in an observable, measurable, relational way—and for the good. For example, I have a friend in the professional world whom I have known a long time. Our paths have crossed through mutual friends and organizations. He has always been a nice guy, very likeable, good spiritual values, smart, and funny. We would have the occasional lunch or coffee. While I have always liked spending time with him, we really never had gone deeper in our friendship or conversation. If I brought up a problem or a struggle I was having, he would be sympathetic, and I would know he cared. But that was as far as the connection would go. He would say, "I'm sorry," or "Anything I can do?" which are certainly not bad things to say. But he couldn't "go there" with me. It was as if he had no experiences he could relate to me.

There are two primary reasons people are like this. Some of them are simply *highly defended*. That is, without being aware of it, they have their own pain that they ward off because they don't know what to do with their feelings and thoughts. They tend to withdraw from people who struggle or difficult conversations or conflict. It is too hard on their system. They are afraid that if they get to close to the painful feelings of another person, their own emotions might be too strong and overwhelm them. So they spend energy keeping things buttoned up and thinking positive. They have difficulty dealing with negative realities.

The second reason people can't go there is because they *haven't had the life experience*. Their hard times have not been severe. Their childhood, love relationships, family, work life, and significant experiences may not have been perfect, but life has been pretty much OK. They don't have any sort of entitled attitude about it, but they just don't have a lot of major struggle in their lives. No stories of the martyr mom, the disconnected father, the drug-addicted brother. They have been spared serious struggle. This is not to minimize their problems, for life isn't totally rosy for anyone. But they have had relatively normal lives. And it is often hard for them to talk about life on the same level with people who have had serious problems.

My friend was the second sort. He was just kind of an innocent guy who hadn't had many difficult experiences in life, that is, until his wife divorced him for another man. Then everything shifted.

His entire world came crashing down around him. My friend was hit from out of the blue by her leaving. He had not seen the signs, partially because people without life experience aren't trained to see the signs in the first place. He was not ready for it. He didn't understand what was going on. He wanted her to stay and work it out. He did everything he could to save the marriage, but she wanted out, and she got out. He was devastated, and it took a long time for him to put his life together again. But eventually, things turned around. Bit by bit, he resumed a normal and stable life.

As he was going through the early stages of his divorce, we started to spend more and more time together with me simply trying to support him. And pretty quickly I noticed he was a different man. He connected. He could go there. We talked about our struggles, our failures, and our fears. We teared up at each others' stories. We prayed for each other. This was a different, new, and better relationship. And it has stayed that way even though his crisis is now over. He is accessible. I call him when I need to talk or vent or whatever, and he is there for me as I am for him. I am not happy his marriage blew up, but I believe God used that crisis to make him a more connected person at levels he was not before. It is a help to remember that even Jesus needed this support in times of distress: "He took Peter and Zebedee's two sons, James and John, and he became anguished and distressed. He told them, 'My soul is crushed with grief to the point of death. Stay here and keep watch with me'" (Matt. 26:37–38 NLT). What is good for Jesus is good for my friend and is good for all of us.

## HARD TIMES BRING US TO CONNECTION

You may be a cave dweller, not opening up in your dark days. Or you may feel guilty, not wanting to burden anyone with your tale of woe. You feel that not sharing burdens helps you and is the way life should be lived. It could help at this point to go over the ways that

God uses difficult times to make you a more relational person—for life.

## GIVING UP SELF-SUFFICIENCY

One of the primary problems of humanity is our bent toward not needing anyone. We want to be a strong, sealed, and self-contained unit, not asking, not requesting, and not requiring anything relational from another person. Having this bent does not mean that you are alone or isolated—you could have many friends. However, you are connected to these friends in your times of strength, but you are isolated from them in your weaknesses.

Leaders, parents, and those who serve as helpers and influencers are especially prone to this disease since many people depend on them. The pressure is there to keep all their problems to themselves and not to let down other people.

There is a reality to that sort of pressure. I work extensively with business leaders, and they have to keep things in place in order to inspire and guide others. At the same time, everyone —from the CEO of a Fortune 500 company to a high-school student—needs to need others. "Yes, there are many parts, but only one body. The eye can never say to the hand, 'I don't need you.' The head can't say to the feet, 'I don't need you'" (1 Cor. 12:20–21 NLT). We are built to need.

One of the things I have noticed in my work with leaders is that giving up self-sufficiency is very difficult for them because of all these pressures. As well, they often gravitate toward leadership because being the strong one is something they do by default. In other words, their career roles fit their inability to let others know they have needs. And it often takes a crisis for them to be able to experience letting others in and the blessing of not being alone. I have worked with executives, pastors, and all sorts of high-capacity individuals who encountered a financial, business, career, or relational tsunami, and it forced them to let people in, similar to my friend's experience during his divorce. But most of them tell me, while they didn't want it to happen, the benefit of letting go of their self-sufficiency made much of it worthwhile.

## CONNECTING TRUMPS FIXING

Many people rush prematurely into being fixed, or rescued, rather than being connected. Sometimes we want the life-problem solved, and we miss God working through the people He brings to us. Presence—the emotional "being there" of others—is ultimately a more powerful force in our lives than if the problem just went away.

By saying this, however, I am also affirming that God is a problem solver. He parted the Red Sea for the Israelites, He rescued Daniel from the lions' den, He fed the five thousand, and He broke Peter out of jail. Today and every day, He finds jobs for people who are laid off. He cures diseases. And He revives dead relationships. Never stop praying for something you desire from Him. Never stop asking for miracles. I have been praying for certain people and circumstances in my life for decades: "Never stop praying" (1 Thess. 5:17 NLT).

But what about now? What if your problem hasn't gone away? What if it will take a very long time? Finally, what if the answer is no? That is very often the reality. In any of these scenarios, we were designed to turn to our relationships simply to bear, tolerate, and handle what we have to handle. And that is when God uses our difficulties to make us relationally based people, rather than solutions-based people—relationships first, solutions second. We need to learn to pursue and receive the gift of connection, understanding, and support from others, and that often does not come naturally. It takes work to move from fixes to connection.

Recently I was working with a team of leaders in a small group setting on matters of personal and life growth. One brought up a business problem he was dealing with. It was a question of how to market a new product his company had engineered. The issue was, as the head of the company, the best marketing approach was to have him become the spokesperson for the product. The product was his, the vision was his, and he knew more about it than anyone else. However, he really didn't want that to be the answer. He didn't think he could communicate the product well or be a good salesperson for it. So he wanted us to help him find a different solution, one that didn't involve him being the up-front person.

The leadership group didn't agree with his request. They said, "We don't see any reason you can't be the guy. You have what it takes." He resisted, and then we drilled down into the personal arena. He began talking about his fear that he didn't fit in with people. He had come from a foster home background, and he had a very difficult early life. He received little social training, so he was always the kid who was picked last in the baseball game. Safety for him was found in the world of the intellect as he has a brilliant mind. He excelled academically and ultimately had a very successful career in engineering. But the old memories of not fitting in had never left him. The group rallied around him once they got the picture. They said, "Sure, you have your eccentricities; who doesn't? But you fit in fine. You have what it takes to promote this. We're for you." They weren't just blowing smoke. These were sober-minded, high-capacity people. They truly thought he had the necessary talent to successfully promote this product. And slowly, as they supported him, he began seeing himself as they did. He began looking for ways to hone his speaking and promoting skills.

What had appeared to be a business problem was, in reality, a relational issue. And once he had solid friends to help him discover who he really was, the business thing began working itself out. In the same way, your hard time means that you need someone to be with you, either connecting and supporting, helping to find an answer, or both.

One thing I see a lot nowadays in this economic climate is people who feel ashamed that they have job or financial struggles. I talk to many individuals who have worked hard all their lives, and now they find themselves looking for another job. I talk to many who have to drastically cut back expenses in order to survive month to month. Many have had to postpone any idea of retirement for the foreseeable future, and they feel that something is wrong with them. They wonder how their neighbors, friends, and family see them. *Am I a loser? Are others going to withdraw from me? Will they not want to be around my negative energy? Are they afraid my situation is contagious?* It can be very painful, especially if you are used to being a high-functioning, achievement-oriented person. In these times and circumstances, we all need relationship to tell us that we are OK, and God sends people to strengthen us: "Therefore, strengthen the hands that are weak and the knees that are feeble" (Heb. 12:12 NASB).

## RECEIVING EMPATHY

A specific type of relational need, empathy can have a very powerful and healing effect on us when we struggle. Empathy is the ability to feel what another person is feeling, especially in the negative: hurt, fear, anxiety, or loss, for example. God designed us to both give and receive empathy, and times of trouble can develop that capacity. Strangely enough, my experience in working with people is that they are pretty good about providing empathy but are often at a loss as to how to receive it. They don't know how to ask for empathy from others, or they simply think it is socially unacceptable to do it. I was speaking recently to an audience, and I was talking about hard times and receiving others' compassion. A man raised his hand and said, "I am in the middle of some very, very hard times, and I want some advice."

"What is your situation?" I asked.

He said, "I had a bad drug problem, and it almost ruined my life. I have been clean and sober for two years now. But I lost my marriage, and I also lost access to my kids. Now I have started a business, and it's going well."

I said, "You have been through a lot. What do you need advice about?"

He said, "I am so afraid I'll make another bad mistake and ruin things again. I think I'll mess my life up again with one bad move. I can't sleep. I get really anxious. I don't make good decisions."

I said, "That is really difficult. What are you doing so far to deal with that?"

He said, "I pray, and I try really hard and use my willpower to stay on the straight and narrow. Will God help me?"

I said, "He will help you. But the plan you are on is not the one He designed for you, and it will not work for you."

He looked confused.

I continued, "God intended us to live with grace as our fuel when we are scared and messing up. That means we need not only to ask Him for help but also to let others know how empty and discouraged we get and ask them for empathy. Your system of willpower is basically the Law. If that worked, the Bible would have ended at Exodus 20, when the Ten Commandments were written."

He still looked confused but thanked me and sat down. I felt like I hadn't gotten through to him.

Later, after the talk, he came up again during the social time and introduced himself. I asked him, "Did what I say make sense?"

He said, "I think so."

I said, "Can you tell me what I said?"

He said, "You said to pray a lot for grace and keep trying."

I said, "I am sorry. I didn't really communicate well with you. That's not what I said. What I wanted you to hear is that you need grace from both God *and* people. Do you have people you can open up to about how difficult things are?"

He said, "I think so, but I haven't done that."

I said, "Go to them and ask them if it's OK if you tell them how scared and discouraged you are and if they will just be caring and empathetic with you."

He said, "I will."

The second encounter seemed to go well with the man. But the point is that this isn't really unusual. I often talk to people who don't know what I mean by "asking for empathy" in hard times, and it requires more explanation. By nature, we often miss our need for empathy or don't recognize it or are afraid of it. But asking for and receiving empathy so that we will feel understood and have the strength to persevere is one thing that God helps us learn in hard times. It may not feel natural or easy at first. Think about the first time you tried to figure out your TV's remote control! It may feel awkward. That's OK. Lots of really good habits and patterns don't start easily. Anything good is worth some effort. God built you to need and benefit from empathy, and your hard times will drive you to that.

## DEVELOPING STRUCTURE

We will never forget 9/11 and its terrors. It was a devastating attack on U.S. soil, and thousands were killed. This became a national trauma and also a national rallying point to be more protective of our country. Psychological researchers learned a great deal from 9/11. They did intense studies on the survivors and on those who had lost relatives. They wanted to find approaches that would help those individuals who had suffered greatly during this event. One of their conclusions was that it was a good thing, as soon as was reasonably possible, for people to return to work and to resume their normal routines of life. This may not make intuitive sense at first, but it worked well. The reason is that working provided a structure for feeling some control and predictability in life. That is, getting to the office at a certain time and engaging in the normal tasks, such as phone calls and meetings, gave individuals a sense that they were not completely helpless or without options in a chaotic world, which is the message the terrorist attack had tried to send.

The same is true with any difficulty you go through. Structure calms us down, gives us a feeling of normal again, and helps us move on. A friend of mine died of cancer last year. His wife, never expecting to be a widow raising kids, went through a great deal of pain and adjustment after he passed away. I talked to her recently and asked how she was doing. She said, "I'm glad I can work. It helps me keep going." While we still need the support of relationship, we can also benefit greatly from daily structure when dealing with a chaotic life event.

While it may seem counterintuitive, relationships can also bring structure in times of crisis. When you arrange to meet with supportive people on a regular basis, with assigned times and dates, that provides a sense of control and predictability. This is why when I am working with someone who is having hard circumstances, one of the first things I prescribe is for them to add structured meetings to their lives. These can be anything from counseling to a small group to a regular coffee date with a close friend.

This requires a little adjustment. Much of our relational life is somewhat spontaneous. We call someone we like when they come to mind and we have lunch with them. But that is simply not enough during difficulties. The mantra I use is: *as stress increases, increase structured support.* Carve out time, probably several meetings and phone calls a week, to make sure you are connected to people who are on your side. These don't have to be very agenda-driven times. Use them to get understanding, validation, prayer, and compassion: "For God is not a God of disorder but of peace" (1 Cor. 14:33 NLT).

There is a final benefit to structured support. We develop more of a sense of internal organization, self-control, and normalcy, whether in good times or bad. It becomes an added competency and skill set. We are able to better accomplish goals and dreams and get the tasks of life done. Just as kids learn about work from the diligence of going to school every day, sitting through classes, taking notes, and doing homework, structured relational support builds strength inside us as well.

## BEING THERE FOR OTHERS ON A DEEPER LEVEL

God also uses our struggles to help us give to others who may have similar problems at a future time. There is no more valuable gift than having a friend who has really "been there" share your grief. Countless times I've heard of a person who is having a specific life circumstance unexpectedly meeting someone who has had a similar experience but is some distance further down the road. And it seems as if they begin communicating on an entirely different level, almost a language of their own. One will say, for example, "How are the mornings? You know about that? They are the worst." To an outsider, it may sound like discouragement, but it is a very healing and identifying moment: *you've been there, and you get it.*

Jon and Cindy experienced an unspeakable tragedy about a year ago. Their young adult daughter was killed in a car wreck. It was an unbelievably devastating blow to them and to their entire community. Parents are not supposed to outlive their children. Our families attend the same church, and we were able to have some measure of contact with them over the months after the death. I ran into Cindy recently and asked how she was doing. She told me two things that made me pause and think for a long time. First, she said, "The pain is still there, and I still miss my daughter terribly, every single day. But I have been surrounded by my close friends through this. I have a few soul mates who are walking through this with me. Over and over again, they have just let me feel my grief and talk about it. They show up for me. And they have made all this easier to bear."

Then she said, "Also, for some reason, I have lately found myself surrounded by people who have had similar losses to me. But these individuals are newer to the process and have no idea where to turn or what to do. Their lives are turned upside down. They just show up in my life and want to talk to me. And when we talk, they tell me it helps. The things I have experienced and learned on my journey are apparently providing some hope and a path for them in some way."

All these principles have made a profound difference in my own life. Recently I went through some health problems that were disturbing for me. I developed vertigo and tinnitus (ringing of the ears) with no apparent cause. I went the normal route of seeing my family physician, then moving to specialists: an ENT, an audiologist, and others. When no answers came, I was finally referred to a neurologist, who scheduled an MRI to see if I had a brain tumor. If you have had that sort of spectre for yourself or your family, you will understand the anxiety and fear I felt. But I had several very close friends who stayed in touch during all the weeks of tests from the family physician to the neurologist. My wife and my friends were there to listen, talk, and pray while I went through the process. It was not easy, but I can't imagine going through that alone. The MRI came out negative. However, had it been bad news, the people in my life were ready for that possibility, and they were also readying me as well. They would have walked with me through it. Find your people and let them in.

# CHAPTER 11

# THE GOD OF FAITH WHEN THERE ARE NO ANSWERS

Possibly the most difficult question you'll ask during a struggle is, "What if I can see no good coming from this?" When there is no revelation from the sky. No evident purpose to your pain. No sense of "Oh, that's the reason! Now I see why I had to go through this!" Nothing. There is just you and the problem. This the hardest experience of all.

Look at the contrasts. It is difficult enough to encounter a major struggle even if it is resolved successfully, and you get a better job, recover your health, or reconcile an important relationship. But it is even more difficult to suffer greatly, and it doesn't go away. Sometimes, at least we see the reason for our pain—a miracle results as someone in your life comes to faith in Christ because of your trial, or you learn a valuable lesson about life and God. But when there is simply a veil of mystery with no evident answer, suffering is much harder to bear. What's the purpose? What's the reason? Is all of this a random, disappointing universe? Again, where is God?

The Bible identifies and expresses this concern and does not gloss over it. Psalm 88 is well known as the only psalm in the Bible which actually provides no hope. While many psalms begin with hard times, they mostly end with praise and hope in God. Not this one:

> O LORD, God of my salvation,
>> I cry out to you by day.
>> I come to you at night.
> Now hear my prayer;
>> listen to my cry.
> For my life is full of troubles,
>> and death draws near.
> I am as good as dead,
>> like a strong man with no strength left.
> They have left me among the dead,
>> and I lie like a corpse in a grave.
> I am forgotten,
>> cut off from your care.
> You have thrown me into the lowest pit,
>> into the darkest depths.
> Your anger weighs me down;
>> with wave after wave you have engulfed me.
>
> You have driven my friends away
>> by making me repulsive to them.
> I am in a trap with no way of escape.
>> My eyes are blinded by my tears.
> Each day I beg for your help, O LORD;
>> I lift my hands to you for mercy.
> Are your wonderful deeds of any use to the dead?
>> Do the dead rise up and praise you?

Can those in the grave declare your unfailing love?

Can they proclaim your faithfulness in the place of destruction?

Can the darkness speak of your wonderful deeds?

Can anyone in the land of forgetfulness talk about your righteousness?

O LORD, I cry out to you.

I will keep on pleading day by day.

O LORD, why do you reject me?

Why do you turn your face from me?


I have been sick and close to death since my youth.

I stand helpless and desperate before your terrors.

Your fierce anger has overwhelmed me.

Your terrors have paralyzed me.

They swirl around me like floodwaters all day long.

They have engulfed me completely.

You have taken away my companions and loved ones.

Darkness is my closest friend. (NLT)


Most thoughtful people can relate to feelings like these: *Why is this happening? It doesn't make sense. It does no one any good.* We have all looked to the sky and asked that question at some point, in some setting. Perhaps you are asking that even now, in an era of planes flying into buildings, global disease, extreme poverty, and financial unrest. But still, why would there be such expressions of seemingly meaningless, purposeless pain in the Bible? Aren't we supposed to get hope from God?

I think that we are supposed to experience hope in suffering because it's hard to go on without hope. But hope is impossible unless we experience empathy and identification. We cannot feel hopeful that things will be OK unless someone understands what we are going through and gets it. And I think that one of the purposes of this psalm is to let us know that it's OK to wonder and not see the good purpose in our pain. It is normal. It is a human thing, not a bad thing. Read Psalm 88 again and say to yourself, "God says it's OK for me to feel the way I feel. He isn't mad or disappointed in my lack of faith. He is with me, and He wrote about my experience." I am so glad these verses are in the Bible, just so we can know He identifies so deeply with us.

## THE BIBLE DESCRIBES ALL OF REALITY

Over my years of counseling, speaking, and media appearances, I have heard so many people say, in one form or another, that they see the Bible as basically being a collection of positive and inspiring sayings. They expect to read uplifting and affirming words of encouragement and happiness. They open up the pages to experience that happiness. I can't blame anyone for wanting that because we all need positive encouragement. And I do believe that the Bible gives a real hope that will sustain us in God's love and ways. But the problem is that in providing hope for us, God also points us to our very need for Him and His help. While the Bible contains many, many positive and encouraging stories and sayings, it also speaks a great deal of pain, suffering, and negative things. You read about the horrors of violent death, murder, rape, and child sacrifice. Within the first three chapters of Genesis, the world is corrupted by the Fall, and the problem is not cleared up until the final verses of Revelation. In fact, the thrust of the Bible is God's redemption of His alienated people over thousands of years with the centerpiece being the unjust suffering, torture, and execution of Jesus. These are negative realities. But we have to understand these negatives because they point us to how much we need God.

Think about it this way: without the negative realities the Bible describes, Christianity would basically be diluted into a Prozac-like religion. When we're down, we'd just pop an encouraging verse and we'd feel up again for a few hours. Again, encouragement is something everyone, myself included, certainly needs during tough times. But we need more than encouragement because our situation is worse than our simply being down. Our situation is *absolutely hopeless without God*: "Find rest, O my soul, in God alone; my hope comes from him" (Ps. 62:5 NIV). It's not a situation of us moving from good to great. Our lives will fail in the most important aspects of existence if God is not a part of it.

And without the death and resurrection of Christ, in all its ugliness and glory, we are objects of pity:

> And if there is no resurrection of the dead, then Christ has not been raised. And if Christ has not been raised, then your faith is useless and you are still guilty of your sins. In that case, all who have died believing in Christ are lost! And if our hope in Christ is only for this life, we are more to be pitied than anyone in the world.
> —1 Corinthians 15:16–19 (NLT)

I remember when Mel Gibson's *The Passion of the Christ* came out; I called the parents of our sons' friends and asked if I could take them in our minivan to see it. These boys were all between eleven and thirteen years old. I focused especially on our unchurched friends because I thought it was such a powerful description of the meaning of Christ's death. The parents all agreed, and in fact, we ended up taking two groups. The kids seemed to respond positively to the movie, and we had some pretty meaningful discussions about religion. But a couple of the parents were a little hesitant because of the explicit violence portrayed. I could understand. If you haven't been exposed to a lot of the Bible, it can be shocking to really read what it says. But it's there for a reason.

In addition to these negative realities, the Bible also describes great and positive realities. Ultimately God wins. The universe ends up the way He wants it to. And how much more meaning does that have for us when we see that He understands our struggling circumstances and shows us the way?

I spent a lot of time in this section on the idea of negative realities of our lives and in the Bible, not only to show that it's normal but also to explain the deeper part of what God is doing with us in those times that make no sense: He is growing us up in faith. And faith is one of the most useful and valuable capacities we can develop in life.

## THE WALK OF FAITH

What is faith? It is the hardest and most beneficial step that people have taken for thousands of years, and it has worked for them because God designed it to work for all of us. Faith is trusting God for your problems and for your life. Faith is trusting that He wants what is best for you. You will be most successful in a tough life when you come to a point in which you place your trust in God's unseen care rather than in what you see around you. Faith is the only way to keep difficult times from causing you to despair or give up.

The life of faith creates a genuine paradigm shift for most people. In faith we realize the possibility that even if the situation does not change, life can be good. That is all any of us really want in the first place. We want to know that life is good. Not perfect but good. Not problem-free but good. Good in some way that we did not anticipate. Good in some way that connects us to God, others, and our purposes in life. We want to experience joy even when our situations do not get better. Faith is not bound by situations because God sees beyond our situations. Let me repeat it, for we need to remember this: faith in God creates the possibility that even if our situations do not change, life can be good.

The Bible describes faith in this way: "Now faith is the assurance of things hoped for, the conviction of things not seen" (Heb 11:1 NASB). That is, faith requires darkness, blindness, and stumbling around. If the job or relationship magically got fixed, that would be wonderful. But that would be "things seen," not "unseen." The answers and solutions would be staring us in the face. Then every time we encountered a speed bump or a train wreck and we could see instant results, we would not be able to be people of faith. We would experience God as a genie who lives to solve our problems and make things right for us.

None of us should roll over and accept pain too quickly. We should protest it, address it, talk with our friends about it, deal with it, try to resolve it, and ask God for help with it. That makes sense. But there are just those times in which things aren't changing and may never change.

So a good and simple working definition of *faith* is "putting trust in God." That is, to depend on the reality that who He says He is in the Bible and how He has revealed Himself in reality is the way He truly is. When you put your trust in God, you do two things: you cast your cares on Him, and you live in His ways. That is how faith operates.

Faith has the same dynamics in relationships that it does with God. For example, when a wife calls a husband at work and asks him to bring home some vegetables to cook with dinner, she has faith that he will get them to her in enough time to cook them along with the rest of the meal. Having faith in him means that she has to go out on a limb. She has to take a risk. The risk is that she doesn't postpone dinner to go to the grocery store for the vegetables. She doesn't go to the freezer and defrost a plan-B vegetable, just in case he doesn't come through for her. She depends on him to do what he promised. In the same way, faith in the unseen God in uncertain times is taking a risk. It is saying, "I believe You are who You say You are. And though I do not understand my circumstances, I place my trust in You." It is that simple. It's not easy; in fact, it's often very difficult. But it is simple.

# THE OBJECT OF FAITH

Faith in God has to do with trusting His character. He is the object of our faith and trust. He describes Himself and His character all through the Bible, where we see His grace, His power, and His love. The promises in the Bible are a testament to God's character. As people have done for centuries, we can stand on the promises He makes to us in His Word, of which these are a small sampling:

> The LORD gives his people strength. The Lord blesses them with peace (Ps. 29:11 NLT).

> Love the LORD, all you godly ones! For the LORD protects those who are loyal to him, but he harshly punishes the arrogant (Ps. 31:23 NLT).

> But seek first his kingdom and his righteousness, and all these things will be given to you as well (Matt. 6:33 NIV).

> And this same God who takes care of me will supply all your needs from his glorious riches, which have been given to us in Christ Jesus (Phil. 4:19 NLT).

> I will never fail you. I will never abandon you (Heb. 13:5 NLT).

When you look at these promises, it sometimes doesn't make sense on a perceptual level. It may seem that in your present situation, God is not providing peace, giving protection, meeting your needs, or doing much for you at all. While the purpose of this book doesn't allow for an in-depth answer to the problem, there is a guiding principle that can help: God determines the nature of what He promises to us, and we are to seek Him to understand that. He will "supply all your needs," but He knows the nature of your needs and how He will meet them. For example, if you need to take care of your family in an economic downturn, God may have some other way to provide for them than the particular job or industry you have been operating in. If you need a supportive connection with someone you can feel loved by and your spouse is alienated from you, God may have a small group or community to bear you up and walk through life with you. The best stance is to ask God for His resources, but to keep an open mind to His ways of executing His promises.

Having said that, it's important to understand that the object of faith is not having the outcome we desire. God may have a solution or path for us that we don't anticipate. So we are to direct our faith toward His character, rather than toward what we wish for. Wishes and desires are a good thing; they keep us in touch with our hearts and our passions, and they help direct us to what is important in our lives. Talents, gifts, careers, and great relationships start with wishes and desires. Never hold these back. At the same time, however, your heart, soul, mind, and strength must bow before God Himself and trust that He knows what path is best for you.

You may be thinking, *But all this information and all these ideas about where God is do not change my situation. I still don't have a job, relationship, good health, or any other problem fixed. Things aren't OK.* Let me rephrase this from a faith perspective, to help improve the outlook: *I still don't have a job, relationship, good health, or any other problem fixed. I am working hard and praying hard to change things. But because I trust God, even if my situation does not change, my life can still be good.* This is not denial or resignation. It is not defeatism. It is not some feel-good phrase. It is, actually, the only answer to problems that are beyond our strength to bear. Instead of trying to change things all by ourselves and instead of trying to force God to fulfill our wishes, we put ourselves in His hands, walk in His ways, and find that life can be good—*even with our problems.*

As everyone has experienced during the recent economic downturn, there are lots of people with severe financial problems—the scale of which we haven't seen in this generation. In the past couple of years, many people have been laid off or had their homes foreclosed on or lost most of their net worth almost overnight. You may be in this situation as well, or at least you probably have several friends who are in financial trouble. Is there an answer? We can talk all day about what it all means, but no one knows for sure. We're still in the middle of it. And we may never know God's purpose in all this on this side of the grave. So without an answer, what do we do?

We must exercise faith. We don't pretend we're fine. We don't deny it. But we trust in Him. The result is a double benefit: "And it is impossible to please God without faith. Anyone who wants to come to him must believe that God exists and that he rewards those who sincerely seek him" (Heb. 11:6 NLT). First: we please God. Second: He rewards us in some form or fashion.

This is what I have seen in so many of my friends who have been severely affected by the downturn. They are certainly doing all they can to find jobs, money, and solutions. But at the same time, they are trusting that God loves them and will take care of them.

C. S. Lewis describes faith during dark days in a similar way. In his well-known book, *The Screwtape Letters*, a senior devil is training his nephew on how to undo spiritual growth in humanity. Screwtape explains to Wormwood the dangers of letting people suffer without seeing answers from God:

> He wants them to learn to walk and must therefore take away His hand; and if only the will to walk is really there He is pleased even with their stumbles. Do not be deceived, Wormwood. Our cause is never more in danger than when a human, no longer desiring, but still intending, to do our Enemy's will, looks round upon a universe from which every trace of Him seems to have vanished, and asks why he has been forsaken, and still obeys.[1]

There are those times that we don't get it, when every trace of Him seems to have vanished. But God has not vanished; He is very present though He may be beyond our experience at that time. We have all been through this, and you may be going through this now. If that is where you are, ask Him for more faith. Ask Him to develop and grow your faith. Like the father of the demon-possessed son who cried to Jesus, say to Him, "I do believe, but help me overcome my unbelief!" (Mark 9:24 NLT). He will help you. He will increase your ability to trust Him, to be calmed, and to "Cast all your anxiety on him because he cares for you" (1 Pet. 5:7 NIV).

## THE ANSWER IN JOB

We cannot really understand where God is when things don't make sense without looking at the life of Job. A good and righteous man loses his family, possessions, and health. He suffers terribly and is given little help from his friends. Job, however, does not pretend. He doesn't act like things are wonderful. He protests the entire meaning of his life:

> Why wasn't I born dead?
>> Why didn't I die as I came from the womb?
> Why was I laid on my mother's lap?
>> Why did she nurse me at her breasts?
> Had I died at birth, I would now be at peace.
>> I would be asleep and at rest.
> —Job 3:11–13 (NLT)

As with Psalm 88, you may identify with this deep despair: *better to not be here than continue this pain.* It is the mark of someone who is beyond the end of his rope. And if you are in this state, you need compassion, help, and support from God and safe people. It is not a time to try to go it alone.

However, Job's story continues with a great deal of dialogue between himself and his friends. The subject is *What is the reason for my suffering?* Is it his own sin and misdeeds? A lack of faith? The friends present different unsatisfactory solutions. However, the closest thing to a final answer in the story happens near the end, when God thunders from the whirlwind:

> Where were you when I laid the foundations of the earth?
>> Tell me, if you know so much.
> Who determined its dimensions
>> and stretched out the surveying line?
> What supports its foundations,
>> and who laid its cornerstone
> as the morning stars sang together
>> and all the angels shouted for joy?
> —Job 38:4–7 (NLT)

For several chapters, God sets out example after example that point out this basic truth: *He is the Creator with His own purposes, and we are His created.* He does not explain why there is suffering beyond that. Instead, He describes a mystery. It is the mystery of worshiping God who is far beyond us yet still intimately connected to us. His ways are truly beyond our ways.

In his excellent book *Disappointment with God*, Phillip Yancey provides a very helpful clarification of what the book of Job is really about:

> . . . regardless of what Job thinks, God is not on trial in this book.
> Job is on trial. The point of the book is not suffering: Where is God

when it hurts? The prologue dealt with that issue. The point is faith: Where is Job when it hurts? How is he responding? To understand the Book of Job, I must begin there.[2]

This makes sense. It can sound somewhat harsh, as if God is answering our protest by putting us in our place. But that is not what I think is going on. I think God's answer is full of grace and help for us. He is saying, in effect, *Let it go.* Let go of taking on a burden of understanding all the mysteries you aren't equipped for. Let go of the pressure of trying to be God and think like God. Rest, trust, and be His creation and His child. That is the great design.

We have two Labrador retrievers that we love. Heidi and Casey have given our family many years of companionship and fun. But they don't understand why we have to leave the house to go to work or school. They stand there quietly with their sad Lab eyes, near the front door, watching us walk out. I am somewhat codependent with our dogs, so I often try to explain matters to them: "Girls, we have to leave because there are things we need to do. But we'll be back." As of yet, the dogs have given me no sign of "Thanks for the explanation, Dad." They just keep looking at me with those sad eyes. So I feel a little sad for them as well. I imagine that's how God may feel when we look at Him with our sad eyes, not understanding the meaning of our struggles.

Pardon me if it seems I am trivializing a crisis you may be in; that's not my intent. It's just a simple explanation of the reality that we are ultimately better off accepting mystery—being the created and living in faith—than striving to figure everything out. We then have the energy and wherewithal to actively pursue those things that can help our lives and situations, rather than having the power-drain of obsessing forever about mysteries that will not develop us.

# "I DON'T KNOW" IS OK

As someone who lives in faith, make it OK for yourself to say, "I don't know why." If you don't know why you struggle as you do, that is just reality. Don't be codependent with God, ascribing motives to Him so you'll feel better or so other people will like Him better. I hear this a lot, and I don't think it helps anyone. For example:

- Instead of saying, "I lost my job because I needed to learn humility," say, "I don't know why I lost my job, but I am putting my faith in God and working hard."

- Instead of saying, "My husband left me so that I can teach others about divorce," say, "I don't know why God allowed this, but I am putting my faith in Him and getting as much support and growth as I can."

- Instead of saying, "I have a heart problem so that I'll slow down," say, "I don't know why I have this, but I am putting my faith in God and taking care of myself and my family better."

- Instead of saying, "My child is doing drugs because God wants me to learn a lesson," say, "I don't know why God allowed this, but I am putting my faith in God and focusing on her recovery and our family's health."

If you are sure of God's motives, if God has revealed His purpose behind your pain as He did with Joseph, that is a different matter. But "I don't know" is no sign of a lack of faith or resentment toward God. In fact, not knowing but trusting at the same time is a mark of great faith in His love and care for you. It is accepting your position as the creature, instead of insisting on being the Creator. God sometimes does reveal over time the redemptive meaning behind our struggles as we are better able to look back over the seasons of our lives with more perspective. But sometimes He does not. Sometimes we must trust.

## GROWING YOUR FAITH

If you are to understand this last where-is-God-in-difficult-times answer—that He is developing your faith—then you need to know how to do that. Faith is not constant, nor are you born with great amounts of faith. It must be grown and developed over time.

Some of us have young faith, some broken faith, and some mature faith. Since it is such a valuable capacity, it's helpful to know how it grows. The Bible explains that faith was designed to be dynamic and developing:

- FAITH CAN GROW: "Nor do we boast and claim credit for the work someone else has done. Instead, we hope that your faith will grow so that the boundaries of our work among you will be extended" (2 Cor. 10:15 NLT).
- FAITH CAN BE STRONG INSTEAD OF WEAK: "For though I am far away from you, my heart is with you. And I rejoice that you are living as you should and that your faith in Christ is strong" (Col. 2:5 NLT).
- FAITH CAN FLOURISH: "Dear brothers and sisters, we can't help but thank God for you, because your faith is flourishing and your love for one another is growing" (2 Thess. 1:3 NLT).

In tough times when we don't understand God's dealings, a strong faith is vital. You may not have enough faith to navigate through the difficulty you are experiencing. It may simply be too huge or overwhelming. You are not alone. Many people have the same experience. Here is what I have studied and experienced as the key elements of growing faith.

## HUMBLE YOURSELF

Faith grows when we assume the position of one who can't do it all for himself. That means we go to God, follow Him, and ask Him for help: "So humble yourselves under the mighty power of God, and at the right time he will lift you up in honor" (1 Pet. 5:6 NLT). Humility is not looking at yourself as a worm but simply *looking at yourself as who you are in reality, both good and bad.* You are someone with strengths and weaknesses, like anyone else. But your strengths cannot totally compensate for your weaknesses. They do not erase them. Instead of trying to be God and keep things all together, God designed you to look to Him for help in a difficult world.

Humility also means giving up the position of entitlement. *Entitlement* is believing that we deserve or are entitled to special treatment simply because we exist. For example, someone might say, "I deserve this marriage, this special treatment, this better job, or this longer break." When you probe further into personal entitlement and ask, "Why do you deserve these things?" people will often say, "Because I have a right to them" or "Because I've had a hard time." Some people may think to themselves, *Because I'm special,* and really crazy people will actually say it out loud! Entitlement is linked to a proud, grandiose, or narcissistic tendency in people. They perceive themselves to be above the rest of society.

The reality, however, is that usually a great deal of grace combines with a great deal of effort to create good marriages (for example), not entitlement or pride. And that is the way it is with faith and God as well. We come to God in humility not because He owes us any sort of special treatment. He is full of grace and help. But His help is dispensed far more when we come in humility and need than when we come to Him with an attitude of *You owe me.* "God opposes the proud but favors the humble" (James 4:6 NLT).

I find this very useful for people in their marriages. When they are at odds, one will tend to throw up the entitlement flag: "You owe me more attention, time, space, freedom, or respect," for example. That spouse doesn't realize how it pushes away the other person who then thinks: *I owe you what? So I am now obligated to do these things? Where did I sign up for that list?* Then love becomes an obligation and a duty to fulfill, instead of being a connection out of compassion and care. I will coach them to change what they say. Instead of saying, "You owe me," or "I deserve," I ask them to say, "I need": I need this from you. I am lonely and want more connection with you. I feel hurt and need more gentleness from you. I need for you to listen to my opinions and respect my choices.

Do you see the difference? It is the difference between need and demand, between humility and entitlement. Need draws the other person in while entitlement pushes away. It is the same in our relationships with people as it is in our relationships with God.

The disciples had similar attitudes about growing their own faith. Watching Jesus, they knew they needed more of His kind of trust in the Father. The story goes this way:

The apostles said to the Lord, "Show us how to increase our faith."

The Lord answered, "If you had faith even as small as a mustard seed, you could say to this mulberry tree, 'May you be uprooted and thrown into the sea,' and it would obey you!

"When a servant comes in from plowing or taking care of sheep, does his master say, 'Come in and eat with me?' No, he says, 'Prepare my meal, put on your apron, and serve me while I eat. Then you can eat later.' And does the master thank the servant for doing what he was told to do? Of course not. In the same way, when you obey me you should say, 'We are unworthy servants who have simply done our duty.'"
—Luke 17:5–10 (NLT)

At first glance, this story may sound harsh or unloving. The master doesn't even thank the servant? God isn't even polite enough to say "good job" when we work hard? We know that this is not His nature. Two chapters later in a different story, Jesus says, "'Well done!' the king exclaimed. 'You are a good servant. You have been faithful with the little I entrusted to you, so you will be governor of ten cities as your reward'" (Luke 19:17 NLT). No, the parable above simply has a different point to it. The point is that we are to take on the attitude of service and humility, not entitlement. Faith grows when we take the humble role.

## PRAY AND ASK FOR WHAT YOU NEED

It sounds a little too obvious, but it is necessary. The second step of faith development is to engage in the dialogue of prayer with God and ask Him for help in your situation. It is called *supplication*, a particular type of prayer. In a sense, asking God is putting yourself at risk. You are saying, "I really can't do this for myself, and I need your help and guidance." When you pray, you are bringing your difficulty, your pain, your confusion, and your need into relationship with God.

"Ask and it will be given to you; seek and you will find; knock and the door will be opened to you" (Matt. 7:7 NIV). Sometimes people feel a sense of disloyalty to God if they ask specifically, authentically, and even emotionally for what their hearts desire. They think, *I should be happy and joyous over all the things He has given me.* Certainly, we should celebrate the good. But God doesn't need us to rescue Him. He knows our needs. He requires this sort of prayer from us for our sake, not His. He knows it helps us and is healthy for us to ask. He wants the connection even if it's about our deprivations and needs.

Now that Barbi and I have teenagers, I have come to understand that when I get a text from them, it is usually about extending a curfew or needing money. That's fine. That's my job as a parent, to provide the resources my kids can't. God is the same way. Asking is part of faith development.

# DO YOUR PART

In addition to humbling ourselves and asking God to meet our needs, we are also to figure out and execute our own tasks to accomplish our goals. There is generally some role to play, some effort required, for us to be part of God's process of taking care of ourselves. He has His job to do, which is to provide those things we can't provide: bringing in a company to have a job opening for you, many years of training for the right doctor for your surgery, or moving supportive people to walk through a distress or loss with you. Ours is to do whatever we can: interviewing people and companies for jobs, researching the doctors who are in the particular specialty needed, or calling and asking some safe people for help. The mantra of "let go and let God" sounds great, but it doesn't mean, *don't take any responsibility or action; let God do it all*. It actually means, *let go of the responsibilities God will carry*.

There is a balance between our part and God's part in faith. Paul says it this way:

> Dear friends, you always followed my instructions when I was with you. And now that I am away, it is even more important. Work hard to show the results of your salvation, obeying God with deep reverence and fear. For God is working in you, giving you the desire and the power to do what pleases him.
> —Philippians 2:12–13 (NLT)

There are two types of *work* at play here: We are to work hard. And God is at work. It is a project of colaboring. Faith and hard work go together.

## WAIT PATIENTLY

We need to give our schedules to God, for He knows the timetable. It is His; it belongs to Him. It's certainly good to pray for a time-critical crisis and to be very honest with God about the time elements. I have a list of time-based needs in my prayer notebook. But at the same time, we have to surrender to His timing: "Wait patiently for the LORD. Be brave and courageous. Yes, wait patiently for the LORD" (Ps. 27:14 NLT).

I have been touched and moved by people who wait patiently. I am not very good at waiting though I am better than I used to be. But there are heroes in this field. I have a friend, Gary, a corporate executive whose teenage son has had extremely complex and serious medical problems for the last year. He sends regular e-mails to his friends to keep us updated. Their experience is a true roller-coaster. One week I read a praise report that the treatments are improving things. The next week, it's a prayer request because of a setback. Next week will have a celebration but the next week, another setback and on and on. When I talk to Gary, he is a rock. He doesn't deny the toll on his son and his entire family; they become weary and exhausted. But he truly knows how to wait patiently.

Another aspect of patience is to be emotionally present. While you are waiting on God for help, you are to be emotionally in touch with what is going on. This means really embracing your feelings about your circumstance: fear, anxiety, sadness, or anger, for example. Your emotions are there to keep you aware of your internal world and your external situation. They serve as a signal to help you know how you are doing. If they are too strong and disabling, that means you are to reach out and get help, for example. So stay in touch with them.

It's not easy to feel distress and still be patient about an impending mortgage payment that you don't have the money for. It's simpler to either be anxious and give in to worry and obsession or to go to the other side of the coin into some sort of spiritualized denial and, in the service of patience, pretend to yourself that you have no anxiety. I often see this in people who come from family settings in which they couldn't talk about negative realities, such as loss, failure, or hurt. They say things like, "I'm waiting on God; it's going to all be fine. I'm fine, just fine. Really, I'm great. Isn't God good?" Sometimes they nod their heads and smile very brightly as if to soothe themselves on the inside that things are really OK. It's painful to watch because I care about them and know that the distress they feel has no place to go. Their patience is a good thing, but they are out of touch with their very hearts. The wise man said that instead of pretending, "Sorrow is better than laughter, because a sad face is good for the heart" (Eccl. 7:3 NIV). That is being emotionally present while you are enduring hard times.

Jesus' experience provides us with the most stirring example of this capacity, just before His crucifixion:

> He took Peter and Zebedee's two sons, James and John, and he became anguished and distressed. He told them, "My soul is crushed with grief to the point of death. Stay here and keep watch with me" (Matt. 26:37–38 NLT).

> Then Jesus left them a second time and prayed, "My Father! If this cup cannot be taken away unless I drink it, your will be done" (Matt. 26:42 NLT).

In the first passage, He is clear about the pain and distress He is in. It is acute. There are probably no words for us to really understand His experience. He was, as none of us could ever be, emotionally present. And in the second passage, though He would rather the cup pass from Him, He takes the position that God's will be done, not His own. That is the way of patience, of allowing God to be in charge of the situation and the outcome. That is the balance, and that is the goal.

How long do you have to wait for God to answer? The answer is, *as long as it takes.* Remember that there are many things going on in your circumstance that only God is aware of, and you are not. The answer may come immediately. It may take a long time. And the answer may even be no. I have experienced all three, and I'm sure you have as well. But we are to stay diligent in our part while we look to His answer. During a seminar where I was speaking, I talked to a woman who waited years for her husband to admit he had a substance abuse problem and get help. She didn't put her life on hold, but she waited. She stayed for him, the marriage, and the kids. She took a strict zero-tolerance stance toward the drugs and required him to move out. She did a lot of her own growth work. She stayed in community. And one day, he hit bottom and sought help. It was a long process of healing for him and for the marriage as well, but this woman left the timing to God and stayed on her own path with Him.

## STAY IN RELATIONSHIP

Speaking of community, here is another significant part of faith development that comes from Jesus' words in that same previously quoted passage, Matthew 26: in His dark times, Jesus sought relationship. He did not suffer silently, stoically, or in isolation. He humbly asked Peter, James, and John to be with Him. He confessed the reality of His anguish to them. He sought their presence and support. And He did the same in His prayer to the Father. He was honest, humble, and He asked for what He wanted and needed. It is a great thing that Matthew 26 was recorded for us. It is so significant and helpful. We see not only a model of faith, but also we see how to "do faith" in relationship, in connection, and in community.

Faith develops best in relationship as do most things that are important for us. That is why you need to be connected to safe people. This is true whether you are in great times or horrible times. You need continuing, sustained, real connection for the rest of your life. It is the biblical norm, as we discussed in the section on how God is living in those who live with us. Remember that the tougher the times, the more relationship you need. When more is required of you, go out and request more. In my own Life Team—that small circle of people who walk through life with me—it is expected that when one of us is going through a painful time, that person needs to do extra calls, coffees, prayer sessions, texts, e-mails, or whatever. It is understood with us. When you drive your car up in the mountains, it will require more gas sooner. That is a law of physics. The same is true with you personally. Stay in relationship, especially during tough times.

## MARK THE EXPERIENCE

When God shows up and answers, there is one final and important piece of development: mark the experience. That is, we are to remember what happened, to make it part of our lives. We are to celebrate it, speak of it, journal it, and memorialize it. Marking the experience helps faith grow in us so that we are more capable to trust Him the next time difficulty occurs.

The Bible is full of examples of ways to mark experiences. The nation of Israel was shown how to celebrate Passover after their deliverance from slavery. The purpose was to help them "Remember that you were once slaves in Egypt, so be careful to obey all these decrees" (Deut. 16:12 NLT). When God dried up the Jordan River so that they could walk through it and enter the Promised Land, Joshua told them to take twelve stones from the middle of the dry riverbed and make a memorial. Then, as time passed and their children asked about the stones, "Then you can tell them, 'They remind us that the Jordan River stopped flowing when the Ark of the LORD's Covenant went across.' These stones will stand as a memorial among the people of Israel forever" (Josh. 4:7 NLT). We celebrate the Lord's Supper to remember Jesus' sacrifice for us: ". . . do this in remembrance of Me" (Luke 22:19

NIV). It's easy to forget things. Marking the experience helps us remember. The more you remember the things God has done, the more your faith is built up.

Recently, a good friend of mine, Dave, was diagnosed suddenly with a rare heart condition. With no warning, he collapsed. He was rushed to the hospital where he was given a one in one-hundred-thousand chance of survival through the necessary surgery. It was a frightening time for his family, friends, and the entire community. However, he came through it and recovered. I don't know what percentages qualify for being a technical miracle, but it is close enough for me. When Dave returned to normal life, people were all over him. When Barbi and I saw him at church, we asked him to have lunch with us to tell us the story. However, during all this time, I was also hearing stories from others about Dave as well. It was "Dave month" for a while, and a time of great celebration. This is a mark. Those of us who know and care for Dave will always remember the crisis and the miracle. I know that my faith has certainly grown from this experience.

Infant and child development research supports the idea of the importance of memory, especially emotional memory, in the ways children are supposed to grow. This parallels faith development a great deal. The idea is that one of the first and most important tasks that an infant must accomplish in her young life is to *learn to trust*, which is the definition of faith. As I mentioned in the previous chapter, mothers play a large role in stabilizing infants. One of the things that results from that stabilization and warmth is that the baby develops the capacity to trust her.

Over and over, this process continues throughout the first few hours, days, weeks, and months of life. Babies need a great deal of these being-there experiences with their mothers. It takes a lot of love and grace to resource the infant for all she needs to do. She is busy doing things such as stabilizing, growing at a rapid rate, developing her organ systems, experiencing life outside the womb, and learning to trust. This last aspect is critical. The infant is supposed to experience the reality that relationship is the best place in the world to be. When she is afraid, cold, hungry, in distress, or alone, she learns that Mother, who as far as the baby can tell, equals *relationship* and will be there, and things will be OK. The ability to experience that reality is the establishment of basic trust. From that point, as the infant grows to be a child, she learns that her dad, siblings, and other people are also part of relationship, and they can also bring good things to her. That process is called *internalization*, which simply refers to the reality that babies are taking inside themselves experiential memories of their relationships with their mothers. They are more than snapshot memories. They are emotionally laden memories that, collectively and over years, form the way people look at the world.

When you are at a party and don't know anyone, basic trust helps you feel confident enough to go up and introduce yourself to someone. Many successful internalization experiences tell you, *Relationship works. It is a good thing. I'll find someone who I'll like here.* When you have a problem, it helps you think, *I need to call someone who cares about me,* instead of going inside your cave and trying to do it on your own. More than that, basic trust is essential for making it through life successfully. This ability helps us reach out for support and understanding, learn how to connect with others, know what to do when we have problems, find great friends, fall in love, have a successful marriage, and create our own families. It is the model for our continued spiritual and personal growth. Paul prays that we be "rooted and grounded in love" (Eph. 3:17 NASB). This "rooting and grounding" is about having many experiences of love within the body of Christ to stabilize and strengthen us. Ultimately, basic trust helps us to love and reach out for God Himself: "Yet you brought me safely from my mother's womb and led me to trust you at my mother's breast" (Ps. 22:9 NLT). Trusting your mother, who is flesh, helps you develop the capacity to trust God, who is spirit and, therefore, more difficult to experience and reach out to.

Conversely, when this process doesn't go well, children often grow up with what are called *trust issues*. They don't easily reach out to let others in—it is not a safe experience, based on their internalized emotional memories. Reaching out becomes an experience full of conflict. Or they have a hard time knowing who to trust, and as a result, they let the wrong people in. Or they trust only themselves. This is when healing relationships, from small groups to mentoring to psychotherapy, can help repair the problem and set someone out again with the ability to trust and let others in.

To get back to faith, internalization is a form of marking the experience. Just as having lots of positive interactions in our relationships helps us reach out to others, remembering God's work—including the emotions involved—helps us develop faith itself. When you have a positive experience of faith, like with my friend Dave, it serves as a deposit in your emotional memory bank. The account builds over the process of time when you mark the various experiences and intentionally preserve and celebrate them.

We develop faith through our own personal experiences and also through what we read about in the Bible. When kids learn about Daniel in the lion's den or Noah's ark or Paul and Silas being released from prison, they are shown experiences that serve to build up their faith in a good God who has been taking care of His people for thousands of years. That is one of the benefits of reading the Bible—it is filled with others' stories that can help our own faith.

If you are in a difficult circumstance right now, you may need to build your own faith to help you be sustained through this time. It may be helpful during this period not only to read and record some of the Bible stories that are meaningful in helping faith but also to record those experiences in which God showed up—both in your life and in the lives of those you love. Faith development based on the past can help faith in the present.

## FAITH WHEN THE ANSWER IS NO

There are many times in life in which there is no miracle to celebrate, no parting of the waters. Something has been lost or does not happen the way it should. The dream career doesn't work out. Your financial condition ends up in foreclosure or bankruptcy. The divorce occurs. A young person dies in an auto crash. What about faith then?

There are many people who are in the middle of this right now. Their situation is not in limbo; it is worse than limbo. The nightmare has actually happened, and they are living it. You may be in this situation right now. Your own faith may not be developing. In fact, it may be faltering, and you may not be sure that you can trust a God who says He will take care of you. Or you may have lost or abandoned your faith. Feeling that you have been abandoned by Him, that He has walked away from you, or that maybe He was never there in the first place, you may be responding by leaving the God who, in your mind, left you first.

I wish I could say, "Hang on, the job will come back, the test results will be negative, the marriage will make it, or the young person will come back to life." But that is not always the case. Sometimes, as in many of the examples in this book, the answer is no. So it is important to deal with a particular and specific type of difficult time—the experience of faith in times of great loss. It is one thing to develop faith when we are in the middle of things. It is another when we are at the end of things and the matter is over and done with. What do we do with faith when we hear God say no?

We must follow the same disciplines: humility, prayer, relationship, doing our part, and the rest. The walk of faith is the walk, regardless of the answer. These habits, attitudes, and practices keep us on a path that is ultimately the best for our lives. With that, remember that God sees the entire picture of our lives, the universe, and eternity. We see only a small part from our limited vantage point. "He has planted eternity in the human heart, but even so, people cannot see the whole scope of God's work from beginning to end" (Eccl. 3:11 NLT).

There is, however, one additional aspect of all this that can help you if the answer is a no without any explanation from God: ask Him to help you let it go. When no is no and the door is shut, it is time to accept it and move on. This means asking God to guide you through the process of grief or emotionally accepting what is. God created the grief process for times like these. Open your heart and your sad feelings to Him and the safe people He brings to you. As you let go, you receive the comfort needed in order to regain your bearings in life. Grieving is not a sign that your faith is weak. It is a sign that you trust Him with your sadness that things aren't as they should have been. Psychologically speaking, it is a sign of maturity to be open about your grief and also hold on to God at the same time, all the while knowing He could change things if He so chose. Rather than pretending you are happy when you are not or withdrawing from God in mistrust, the ability to mentally contain ideas that seem contradictory indicates that you are growing and developing in your faith.

# CHAPTER 12

# HARD TIMES ARE THE ACCESS CODE

Recently, I was talking to a neighbor of mine, and the subject turned to personal matters. He told me that he was in the middle of a very difficult custody battle with his ex-wife over their children. He was obviously distraught about it. He already had the kids most of the time, and they seemed to be doing well, but she was in legal proceedings to gain the majority of the custody. It was a heartbreaking situation, the kind in which there are no winners. You just hope the damage can be minimized, especially for the kids. We had several conversations during the following weeks about his situation. I got to know him and the children and the rest of his family. My wife and I visited him at his home. He even showed me legal documents that supported his parenting and the current arrangement.

I am always reluctant to take sides on a relationship problem if the other person is not present to speak for himself or herself. It is just too easy to hear a distorted viewpoint from one individual concerning another's actions or words. So it takes a lot of evidence for me to take sides. My neighbor was not asking me to take sides; however, the more I got to know this man over time, the more it seemed he was a very involved, caring, and competent dad. So one night I told him, "I will pray that you keep custody." We had had some talks about God, so this wasn't out of the blue. He was appreciative, and later that night I asked God to move things so that he would keep the kids.

The next day as I arrived home from work, my neighbor walked up to me before I got out of my car. He said, "My ex's attorney just called. They are dropping the proceedings against me." He had a look of surprise on his face, and so did I. I wanted God to do something, but I didn't expect a twenty-four-hour turnaround! After that, more good things happened. My friend and I began having more spiritual discussions about life and God. Our families became closer, and they began going to church with us. They have since moved away, but we try to stay in touch.

Here is the point to this story: problems can bring us closer to God. When we experience a situation beyond our power to fix or control, the best thing we can do is express it and bring it to God. He moves toward us and responds to our heartaches. The nature of having a struggle itself is an entry point to God. As a computer access code gets us to a site for needed information, problems are access codes to God's presence and help. He is not repelled by our inabilities to keep our lives afloat; He is drawn to it. He opens Himself, His heart, and His help when we are in times of need.

The Bible is full of verses that illustrate this:

The Lord is a shelter for the oppressed, a refuge in times of trouble (Ps. 9:9–10 NLT).

He gives power to the weak and strength to the powerless (Isa. 40:29 NLT).

Don't worry about anything; instead, pray about everything. Tell God what you need, and thank him for all he has done. Then you will experience God's peace, which exceeds anything we can understand. His peace will guard your hearts and minds as you live in Christ Jesus (Phil. 4:6–7 NLT).

Give all your worries and cares to God, for he cares about you (1 Pet. 5:7 NLT).

## PERSISTENCE

God wants to help us and will bear our burdens. You've probably heard it before, and it is true. But let's drill down a little deeper into the dynamics of what that really means for people living in difficult days. The first is the reality that the extent to which we persist in bringing problems to God is the extent to which we connect to Him. We have a need, and He is the resource. Like a hand fits a glove, His strength and presence fit our incompleteness. That is why there are so many passages about praying without ceasing and casting our cares on Him. The nature of His love is that He moves toward struggle and difficulty.

I don't know how many times I have started to pray and began pretty formally, saying, "Thanks for who You are" or something like that and simply had to change directions. In a very blunt way, I had to say, "God, I really hate what is going on, and I need help." This doesn't seem politically correct, but it gets to the need. Certainly there are other times I feel full of praise and wonder. But when I am in a jam, I just start with the problem. I see this in my role as a dad. I want my sons to come to me when they are hurting and bring their pain to me because that is where they are focused in life. I don't need them to say, "How was work today? By the way, I was in a traffic accident."

This need of yours, this difficulty in life, actually draws His love and power to you. This is true on a psychological level. It is how relationships are improved and deepened. Sharing struggles creates intimacy and trust between two parties. It breaks the ice, so to speak. No one really gets close to another if they bypass struggle.

I do a good deal of international speaking as my books are translated into many languages, enabling me to connect with other cultures. Speaking and training on an international level has always been something that has a lot of meaning for me. It also keeps me in touch with the real-life hardships and successes going on in the world beyond the United States. Usually when I receive an invitation to speak in another country, especially from a church or mission organization, they will simply and very directly present the need they are interested in addressing by my speaking there. For example, some relief workers in Sri Lanka sat me down and showed me the effects of the tsunami of 2004. They basically told me that, while the infrastructure was being rebuilt and a lot of progress was being made in rebuilding homes, fishing boats, and businesses, the people were still in a traumatic state. Thousands had suffered unbelievable personal losses, such as spouses, children, and parents. The scale of psychological disruption was unbelievable. Yet there are no licensed psychotherapists in the country. Therefore, the people went to their local pastors with overwhelming needs. These workers asked me if I could help train pastors on a national level in basic counseling principles so they would be better equipped to handle the problems they were facing. How could I say no? The struggles of the country touched me at a deep level, and I went with a team to provide training. The need and the people's situation captured me. And on an ultimate scale and level, that is how God operates with you and me. He is touched and moved by our struggle. The more you present it and the more honestly and humbly you reach out to Him with it, the more you know Him and find Him.

# CREATING A HISTORY IN THE CONNECTION

The Polar Plunge is an Antarctic tourist legend. The guides had us put on bathing suits with our winter clothes on top of those. They took us to a beach and said, "Go!" One by one, we took off the clothes on the beach and ran into the surf. To qualify for the certificate, you have to dunk yourself all the way in before you can run out of the water back onto the beach. I had a couple of second thoughts about it until I saw some ten-year-olds do it; then I had no choice. I can't describe the shock of running into the ice-cold ocean. My nervous system simply shut down for a bit in order to survive it. But for the rest of the trip, those of us on the Plunge talked about the experience as a connector. It became part of our history and legend.

This is how strong emotional attachments are formed between people. When I am working with a couple in counseling, for example, and they are alienated from one another, one of the things I will bring to them is their history. Their present conflict will often give them temporary amnesia over the long sequence of intimate, vulnerable, and positive events they have had with each other. That doesn't mean we ignore the conflict that brought them to my office, but they need the long view to help them reconnect over their shared years together.

There is more to your connection with God than simply coming to Him in your difficult time. You are also creating a relational history with God, one in which you learn His ways, see His work, and experience your journey with Him. In your present crisis, whether health, finance, or relationship, you are forging another experience with God, hopefully one of many. This probably will not be the last problem you bring to Him, as life has its share. But developing the habit of focusing on what you need from Him and learning from Him will deepen your path with Him. There is a phrase I love in the Bible that describes the ancients who were righteous and followed God: they "walked with

God" (Gen. 5:22; 6:9 NIV). Your life can be a continual walk with Him, seeking His ways.

I often recommend to people in their spiritual and psychological journey to record the hard times and what happened with God in those times. How did you approach Him? What were your feelings and experience? How did He show up? How did the matter resolve? These become landmark events in the ongoing process of walking with and being transformed by God, not only in your difficult times but also in the full tapestry of your life on earth.

# CHAPTER 13

# EXPECT THE GOOD

P amela and Dennis are a married couple who live out the principles
in this book. They were just an everyday, ordinary couple whose
everyday, ordinary life skidded to a halt the day Dennis was in a
traffic accident and became a paraplegic overnight. He retained the use
of his arms and upper body, but his legs no longer functioned. Barring
a medical miracle, he will be in a wheelchair the rest of his life.

The few days and weeks after the accident were a blur for them,
oriented toward nothing but the medical aspects: diagnostics, severity
of the injury, and stabilizing him. But when the critical health concerns were over, they were left with a very different lifestyle than they
had dreamed of. They had no idea how to reconstruct life, marriage,
work, and the normal habits and routines that most people take for
granted. But they learned because they had to.

We spent time together dealing with the decisions they had to
make—the changes and the new challenges. There were many of these,
more than most of us can imagine, such as making sure the daily medical regimens were in place, handling the dangers of infections, adjusting

the home to be wheelchair-friendly, and learning to adapt to different ways of transportation. On a more personal level, there were the emotional adjustments as well: the anxiety, the adrenaline surges of not knowing if things would get worse, and the grief over the freedoms and opportunities they had lost. But what makes them heroes for me is that as soon as they began thinking about these matters, they expected God to be good. They thought, prayed, and behaved in that manner. They didn't know how it would happen or what He would do, but they were sure good would come. They were not in some sort of emotional denial of their pain. In fact, they embraced their difficulties and the negative feelings associated with that, and still do. But through it all, and to this day, they continued to look for God's goodness and help.

And they saw it. God showed up in many ways. They saw their church friends spend hour after hour with them, doing everything from cooking meals to cleaning to giving rides to listening and praying. They saw people they knew well become even closer to them than before. They saw Dennis's workplace rally to his side, making arrangements so that he could continue as a valued and productive member of their professional team. They saw their insurance company make decisions that were in their favor, rather than ones that would have put them in financial and medical jeopardy. They saw their own relationship, though more strained and drained through the crisis, continue to grow and deepen. They saw God show up for them with His presence in a way they had not experienced before.

Finally, they have recently begun noticing that people are coming into their lives who need them. These are people who need their experience base, their lessons learned, their care, and their perspective. If you ask them if they would rather the accident never would have happened, I am sure they would say yes. But if you ask them if they experienced good from God, they would not hesitate to say yes, and they would have a great deal of evidence to support their opinion.

The point here is that when we ask, "Where is God?" in the midst of our own personal struggle, part of the answer is that He is found when we expect Him to be good. He becomes more real to us, more personal to us, and more accessible to us. Bear in mind that I am saying to *us*. He is real, personal, and accessible, no matter what we think. But our own attitude and stance toward Him affects how we experience Him and how closely we can work with Him as He supports and guides us.

## WHAT WE KNOW

We know God is good. That is one of the foundational ideas about God's nature we see in the Bible. Over and over again, we read of His goodness.

> Taste and see that the LORD is good. Oh, the joys of those who take refuge in him (Ps. 34:8 NLT).

> For the LORD is good. His unfailing love continues forever, and his faithfulness continues to each generation (Ps. 100:5 NLT).

> Praise the LORD, for the LORD is good; celebrate his lovely name with music (Ps. 135:3 NLT).

> The LORD is good to everyone. He showers compassion on all his creation (Ps. 145:9 NLT).

> Give thanks to the Lord of Heaven's Armies, for the LORD is good. His faithful love endures forever (Jer. 33:11 NLT).

> The LORD is good to those who depend on him, to those who search for him (Lam. 3:25 NLT).

> The LORD is good, a strong refuge when trouble comes. He is close to those who trust in him (Nah. 1:7 NLT).

In the original Hebrew, one of the definitions of *good* is "beneficial." It is something that adds an advantage to our lives. In other words, God's goodness adds benefits to us—benefits that make life work for us, benefits that make us stronger. And in light of the subject of this book, there are also benefits that help us in difficult circumstances. The couple I mentioned at the beginning of this chapter has experienced the goodness, the benefits, of knowing God. So whatever you can do to receive His goodness is worth the effort.

## THE NATURE OF EXPECTATION

Expecting good from God is a part of faith that I dealt with in chapter 6. It is having the corresponding attitude toward God that faith creates: He will do what is best for me based on His love and character. I don't mean that we ignore the realities of our difficult circumstances. Bad times are painful and negative realities. We should be honest about the pain of bad times. There is "a time to cry and a time to laugh. A time to grieve and a time to dance" (Eccl. 3:4 NLT). I do mean that, while we are sad or scared, at the same time we need the capacity to see through the situation to the goodness of God. We know that ultimately God will come through in His own fashion.

## EXPECTING THE GOOD DRAWS YOU CLOSER TO GOD

When we develop the stance of expecting God's goodness, we become more intimate with Him. Basically, the more I understand His goodness, the more I want to be in a relationship with Him. The more relationship I have, the more goodness I experience—in other words, *with God, more is better*. This is a simple relational principle that operates with people and with God. For example, you probably have individuals in your life who bring you goodness. Their warmth, care, wisdom, humor, or empathy simply makes your situation improve. They benefit you. When you come away from an encounter with them, you know you have been filled up, at least for that day. Then there are those individuals from whom you have to recover after a meeting with them. Something about them—a blame issue or a preoccupation with self or their need for you to rescue them from life—keeps you working very hard to survive the encounter! The first group, you look forward to when you see the meeting on the calendar. *Can't wait to catch up with her!* The second, you have to gear up for: *Got to be ready for her.* It's not a difficult question as to which one you want to spend more time with and with which one you have the experience that more is better. It is the same with God. He is not a drain on you. He wants to be a source of goodness for you. As you pray or read your Bible or whatever you do in your connection time with Him, look to His goodness.

I was interviewed on a radio show the other day. The host and I were talking about time management issues from a psychological perspective. A man called in and asked, "These days, with family and work, I'm so busy. I don't have time for a lot of things I need to do. How do I make time to go to church?"

I said, "That's probably the wrong question to start with, and I don't think it will get you where you want to go."

He said, "What do you mean?"

I said, "If you had asked, 'How do I make time for working out or going to the dentist?' I would have given you some tips. But in any relationship that matters, especially our connection with God, when we use the words 'make time,' it brings up obligation and duty. It becomes something we check off our to-do list. And that can get in the way of the benefits of being intimate with someone. I would advise you to unpack your relationship with God. Get out of the duty role with Him, and move into the relational role. What happens at church? I would hope really good things: you worship and feel close to God's love and grace. You cast your cares of the week on Him, and your load is lifted. You learn from a sermon about His ways and plans for you. You meet people who care about Him and care about you as well. In that light, you don't make time for church. You make sure you are going because you want what is there."

With God, more is better.

## EXPECTING THE GOOD CHANGES YOUR ATTITUDE TOWARD YOUR DIFFICULT SITUATION

Basically, when you expect good from God, your attitude or your stance toward your situation tends to change. You become more optimistic, more hopeful. And when you are more optimistic, you are more likely to engage enthusiastically in whatever tasks are needed to help your situation. Optimism—that is, having confidence about the future—is a concept deeply rooted in the Bible, especially during crises and hard times. Though we struggle and suffer, we can be encouraged in our attitude. We know that ultimately God will bring all things to His own good ends:

> Dear brothers and sisters, when troubles come your way, consider it an opportunity for great joy. For you know that when your faith is tested, your endurance has a chance to grow. So let it grow, for when your endurance is fully developed, you will be perfect and complete, needing nothing.
> —James 1:2–4 (NLT)

Research supports the Bible's value of expecting the good with hope and optimism. For example, there is a fairly new school of thought called *positive psychology* that is based on the idea that not everything psychological should be concerned about the diagnosing and treatment of disorders, such as depression, anxiety, and addictions. We should also be researching and developing strengths. Founded by psychologist Dr. Martin Seligman, positive psychology studies the strengths and good habits that help people succeed in life. Researchers in this line of study are concluding that optimism helps children and adults do a better job in reaching their goals and potentials. You see this attitude manifested in how we are to be confident of God's provision and care in our lives: "And this same God who takes care of me will supply all your needs from his glorious riches, which have been given to us in Christ Jesus" (Phil. 4:19 NLT).

I am no pie-in-the-sky, wild-eyed optimist, seeing a blessing in every pain or looking on the bright side of every hurt. The Bible and human experience dictate otherwise—things can be very, very tough. The world is often a place of great pain and anguish at many levels and in many locations. The human race is in real trouble on a micro and macro scale. But given all the negative and positive realities together, given God's nature and the larger perspective over the centuries of our existence, in the final analysis, God tips the scales on the positive side. It is His world, and both now and later, He is the winner. As Jesus said, "I have told you all this so that you may have peace in me. Here on earth you will have many trials and sorrows. But take heart, because I have overcome the world" (John 16:33 NLT).

It's also important to clarify that expecting good from God is more about changing us than changing God. He is who He is: "I do not change" (Mal. 3:6 NLT). His nature, character, and attitude toward us is stable and eternal. He isn't unsure of how He feels toward your tough times. There is a theory in negotiations that says having a positive outlook can make the other person more open to your ideas. But when you look for benefits from God, you are being receptive to the

One who already planned to help you from the beginning of eternity. Though Abraham bargained with God (Gen. 18), God actually knew the end result before it started!

I have some close friends who have a son with a pervasive developmental disorder. This is a category of psychological conditions that include autism and Asperger Syndrome. He has trouble communicating and socializing. When he was first diagnosed, the couple had to begin to grapple with the reality that he would always struggle in life functions, especially relationships. But since he was on the higher end of the category, the couple noticed that with enough support, he often ended up on the normal side of many tasks and activities. However, the boy's school administrators had a habit of not giving him the benefit of the doubt when there was a question of whether or not he could join the mainstream in certain situations or be in special classes. They were so overloaded with the burdens that schools carry, it was easier for them to just say no.

These parents easily could have not pushed and been more resigned to the environments in which their son's school placed him, and no one could have faulted them for that. But they were people of faith who expected good from God. They assumed God wanted more for their son. So they thought, prayed, and behaved in that manner. With the positive and optimistic stance that came from that, they became advocates for their son. They had meeting after meeting at school. They consulted specialists. They enrolled him in special training programs. They hired an attorney at one legal impasse. The result was that the young man is now doing well and almost totally mainstreamed. He will most likely always need some sort of group support structure when he becomes an adult. But that is a far cry from the level at which he could have been functioning. The lesson for us is that when we expect good from God in hard times, we become more active partners with Him in the work that will help us.

# WHEN YOU CAN'T EXPECT THE GOOD: DEALING WITH YOUR DOUBTS

Hard times make it difficult to expect benefits from God. The trials are in your face every day, and God is invisible. Your worries keep you up at night, and God is silent. Troublesome circumstances seem more real and substantial than God does, at least on the outside of things. They speak louder to our five senses than He does. When you simply cannot find within yourself the expectation that God will do good, you are most likely struggling with *doubt*. Doubt is a sense of uncertainty It is a wavering inside as to whether or not God will come through for you. Fortunately, doubt is universal to the human race. If you are doubting and questioning God in your hard time, you are certainly in good company. As we will see, doubt also has spiritual and psychological elements that are helpful to understand in dealing with it.

A friend of mine is a pastor. He told me recently about a life struggle he had quite awhile back when he doubted that God would be good. He and his wife were childless for many years. When they first married, they desired and expected to have kids; they both wanted to be parents very badly. But nothing happened. They investigated and had all the testing you are supposed to have. It was one of those no-answer situations. Everything checked out medically. They did everything right in the procedures of trying to get pregnant. It was literally a mystery.

At first, my friend was patient and expected God to change the situation. Then after some time passed, patience became more difficult. Finally, year after year passed, and he began having severe doubts and even bitterness about God's care for them. It was a horrible, empty time for him. He even came to the point that he felt he should leave the ministry since he could not feel positive about God's benefits to people. How could he lead people spiritually, feeling as he did? It was at that juncture in his struggle that they became pregnant and eventually had two children. God did come through for them. My friend is refreshingly vulnerable about this painful part of his life. He uses it to help people feel that their own doubts are normal.

At the same time, you may be childless yourself and in deep sadness or doubt about God's provision for you. You may say, "Why did this couple get kids and not us?" That is a hard and hurtful situation, and the question is natural to ask. We don't know. All we know is that God has not forgotten you, and He wants good for you in some meaningful fashion.

## A SIGN OF LIFE

In a way, doubt is what this entire book is about. It shows up in the title. *Where is God* in my tough circumstance, when nothing makes sense? Some people, however, worry that their doubt is a sign that they have no faith. If they are not fully confident that God will take care of things, they feel they aren't doing right by God. The reality, though, is that *doubt is not the absence of faith. It is part of faith.*

I see doubt as a sign of life. If you have questions about God's care for you, it means God matters to you. God is important to you, and He is someone who occupies enough space in your mind to bother you when things don't add up. Just as Jacob physically wrestled with God (Gen. 32), doubt is also our way of wrestling with Him.

The same proves true in our relationships. If someone doesn't matter to you personally, doubt is not an issue. If you have some vulnerability with them, however, doubt occurs. For example, when I drive on the freeway, I don't obsess over whether people are going to stay in their lanes and not swerve over and crash into me. I try to do my part and watch out for the crazies, but I don't put a lot of thought into that. I am not involved with those people. I don't doubt or not doubt them. They just don't appear on my radar screen. But if one of my sons is driving and I am in the passenger seat, I become hyper-vigilant. I smash my brake foot onto the carpet on my side of the car if I think he isn't braking fast enough. I tell him, "Slow down!" I get anxious. Sometimes it is for good reason, and sometimes I am being overprotective. But my point is, I am personally involved with my son, so I doubt. I want him to be a good driver, and I want us both to be safe. I am not detached.

Doubting God in your current situation is also a point of contact with Him. When you ask questions— like the why questions that David, Job, and Jesus spoke and were included early on in this book— you are in dialogue. You are not disconnected from God. More contact means more relationship. And as I mentioned earlier, with God, more is better. If you have stopped questioning, it may mean you have given up in despair or resignation. Questions are part of any attachment that has meaning to us.

## IN GOOD COMPANY

History is filled with people who were very devoted to God but who still doubted. When Mother Teresa's private journals were published after her death, the world was shocked by the depth of her painful feelings of spiritual emptiness and doubt. Fully committed to God and her calling to serve the poorest of the poor in Calcutta and eventually winning the Nobel Peace Prize, she could not experience the good from Him. She compared her path toward spiritual confidence in these words:

> Jesus has a very special love for you—for you are so totally His that you live—not you—but Jesus lives in you and through you. He proves His love for the world. As for me—the silence and the emptiness is so great that I look and do not see, listen and do not hear.[1]

Is there a better description of asking the question, "Where is God?" And yet, as far as we can tell from our human perspective, Mother Teresa did life right and is one of the winners.

Theologian John Calvin is one of the most foundational thinkers in Christianity in the last five hundred years. Yet he experienced doubt and saw it as something we all struggle with: "Every one of us knows only too well, from his own experience, our difficulty of believing."[2]

In fact, I personally tend to shy away from individuals who simply seem to experience no doubts at all and appear to be full of faith, 24/7. I try to have a good attitude with them and be open. I try to take what they are saying at face value, and I would never try to read their minds. But sometimes they come across to me as being superior to others who haven't arrived as they have. Other times they seem to be trying to protect God's reputation, so they work hard to reflect well on Him. Others just seem to be a little out of touch with the human condition. I know plenty of people who are much further down the faith road than I am, and even these giants will speak of their own doubts during their hard times. They are both a comfort and an inspiration to me.

# DOUBT'S CAUSES AND CURES

Certainly in your current difficult circumstances, the path for you to be on is that of growing in your faith and learning to expect good from God. This will, in time, decrease your doubts. That simply makes sense. So let's look at some of the causes of doubt to see where you might fit and what you can do about it that will help.

## DISCOURAGEMENT FROM DISAPPOINTMENTS

We are creatures who learn more from experience than we learn from intellect. When life has let you down in significant ways, it can be very disappointing and discouraging. This happens often in the spiritual realm. People ask God for years for things that do not happen. You pray for a healing that does not come. You search for someone to fall in love with, and he does not show up. You ask for your adult child to come to faith, and he shows no signs of interest. Like my pastor friend's infertility experience, after a long time, disappointment is inevitable.

On a psychological level, disappointment trains us to believe that the future will be similar to the past. That is, if I didn't experience the good yesterday or for the past ten years, there is no reason to expect God will bring benefits tomorrow or in the next ten years. We tend to mold our expectations of the future in terms of how we experienced the past. A devoted Christian went through a very difficult job situation. An executive-level professional, he was caught in the resizing process and was let go. What made things harder for him was that for years he had believed that God had given him that position, and it was a perfect fit for him. He loved the job, he was passionate, he was very good at it, and he had a great future. What is more, he believed God had promised him that he would be in that company for a long time, longer than what actually happened. He had, in his experience, heard God specifically make that promise during a time of prayer one night, and he had written it down and held onto it.

I asked him how he was doing with all the losses, and he said it had been hard on a spiritual level. When I asked about that, he said, "God lied to me."

I don't hear that statement from people very often, so it got my attention. I was pretty concerned about how my friend was feeling. I didn't go into a recitation of all the passages that say God tells only the truth. I didn't think that would help him at all, and it would probably make things worse for him. It was a time to draw him out and listen to him. I asked, "Why do you think that?" And he explained to me all that I hadn't known before, about things in his experience that were broken promises from God. We talked some more, and I left it at that.

Over the next several months, when I saw him, I would ask him about his doubt about God's truthfulness. (Actually, it was more than doubt; it was almost a certainty that God wasn't good.) And after a while he told me, "I have been doing a lot of work on this issue. I don't think that anymore." Relieved, I asked how that happened. He then told me that he had figured out that the extreme reaction toward God had more to do with his deep disappointment. Basically, his world had crashed around him, and he was utterly discouraged. The only thing he had been holding on to was the perception of a specific promise from God, and the disconnect was too much for him. However, as he was a man who truly loved God, he stayed in prayer with his doubts and did not dismiss God. And he continued processing his life with safe people who cared about him. Eventually, the connection came back. And his final conclusion was that he had misunderstood what God had said.

This is a complicated matter, but it is common for Christians. I believe God still speaks verbally to His people when He chooses. He is God, and I can find no teaching in the Bible that says He has stopped doing that. I personally have never heard a voice in that physical sense, but many very solid people I know have. At the same time, however, we have to understand that we are human and we make mistakes; sometimes there's a translation problem on our end. Nevertheless, disappointment can cause doubt.

When your hard times lead you to doubt the goodness of God, the last thing you need is for someone to come down hard on you, saying you must not be trying hard enough to have the right attitude, or what's wrong with you? That sort of language only leads to more discouragement. In fact, Job told his friends they were jeopardizing his faith in God by their unkindness in his own pain: "For the despairing man there should be kindness from his friend; so that he does not forsake the fear of the Almighty" (Job 6:14 NASB). If this is your situation, you don't need a pep talk or a criticism to help you expect God's benefits. You need kindness and encouragement. Empty places inside us need to be filled with something that helps, and that is the role of kindness and encouragement. Kindness gives you the safety and grace that supports you. Encouragement gives you the confidence that someone believes in you. The word *encourage* indicates that someone is "putting their courage into" you. You need to get in the presence of God and people who are for you and say to them, "I can't expect the good. Help me." It is their kindness and care that will transform you.

The psychology of this solution simply supports the Bible's teachings here. It is a matter of receiving in relationship what we need emotionally. We can't produce the expectation of God's goodness when it doesn't exist inside. We cannot create what is not there. What we do not possess internally, we must receive externally. That is why other people's kindness and encouragement are so critical. People are the delivery system of God's resources, and we need each other during these times: "And you must show mercy to those whose faith is wavering" (Jude 1:22 NLT).

## A LACK OF EXPERIENCE

Sometimes our inability to expect good from God in our situation is not as much about disappointment as it is a lack of experiences in which God came through for us. It isn't the presence of the negative but the absence of the positive. If there is no memory or lesson to fall back on, it is easy to succumb to doubt. The time I failed so miserably in my job at the children's home was one of the low points of my life. As a young adult, I had to move back in with my parents with my tail between my legs with no job, no money, and no clue as to my future. I empathize with young people nowadays in similar situations. I doubted what God was doing with me because nothing made sense. But that life crisis happened when my faith was still forming. I had started my spiritual life in a renewed way in college, a time with very few serious problems for me, so I had no real background of seeing God take care of something major for me. My faith was simply too new and untested to function well in hard times.

The resolution of this for me is the same as it is for anyone who doubts because of a lack of stories and memories. I stayed on my spiritual path, stayed connected to people who helped me grow and trust, and began collecting more experiences. In other words, I went from no history to a history that had meaning. I was accepted to seminary after they had stopped accepting applications. The money came from an unexpected source. I met people who dramatically changed my idea of God and people and on and on. The point is, if you doubt during your dark times, it may be because you are either a little new to the faith experience or because you have not had a lot of opportunities to trust God and go out on a limb. If that is the case, it is normal to doubt. Don't pretend things are OK, and don't pretend to not doubt. But stay on the path. Grow in your faith. Talk to people of spiritual maturity who care about you. New opportunities to trust will come—financial, relational, medical, and all the rest. You will begin to have your own collection of memories when God came through for you. They will help you look for the next benefit He has for you: "For you know that when your faith is tested, your endurance has a chance to grow" (James 1:3 NLT).

## PSYCHOLOGICAL ISSUES

Doubt can also come from conflicts and hurts in our emotional lives. Psychological issues can often be obstacles to expecting God's goodness in hard times. When we struggle emotionally, sometimes it is hard to see God clearly. We can't experience his hope and peace. The internal receptors don't receive God as they should.

For example, trust issues can play havoc with expecting good things from God. Individuals who have been in significant relationships in which they were betrayed or treated badly often develop an inability to let new people in at a deep level. That inability comes from a doubt in the safety and reliability of others to be compassionate with their vulnerabilities. They have not had good experiences with the character of others. It's a little like the discouragement problem; however, a trust issue takes on a life of its own. It becomes a filter through which we look at life and love. It can dictate how a person approaches relationships. In relational terms, "one can distort many." That is, one significant and important relationship that broke trust can distort many future relationships. The individual generalizes that all people are just as hurtful as the one who damaged him, and it is very hard to break through this. Most of the time, the person who was wounded retreats to a life of self-sufficiency. He may be very caring, but he simply cannot let another person in because he doubts the good character of others.

This often becomes a vertical problem as well since God is easily thrown into the mix of relationships. The fear is that He is just as unsafe as the person who caused the hurt. Sometimes he also ties in the fact that since God allowed that individual to hurt him (as we discussed in chapter 2, Why Ask Why?), by default He is also not to be let inside his heart. I once worked with a client who had been severely abused by her father. Her life was a long struggle, and she worked hard to undo the damage he had done. However, when I mentioned God as a Father, she froze up and reacted to that. It didn't take long to connect the dots that *father* was not an word that evoked feelings of expecting good from God. It brought up terror and mistrust. The solution came in her continuing to work on repairing her "broken trust muscle." She took small relational risks, both with God and with people. She allowed herself to pray on a deeper level with God, telling Him the negatives she felt. And she began to open up to a few safe people about her fears and needs. Eventually, she finished the task, and she was able to more fully trust her heavenly Father who loved her and from whom she could expect the good.

Another psychological issue that I have seen inhibiting people is depression. Depression is an emotional disorder that causes a person to experience a number of distressful symptoms, such as feelings of hopelessness, a negative self-image, energy problems, and sleeping or eating struggles. It can be very painful and debilitating, and it can simply sap the life out of a person. It is much, much worse than discouragement. It is closer to actual despair. Depression can have many causes, ranging from biochemical problems in the brain to trauma and unresolved grief. Because of the negative and dark nature of depression, it can also cloud a person's ability to expect good from God or from anything or anyone. It's easy to see how a depressed person, who, on top of that, has a hard-life circumstance, will have problems hoping for something positive. The good news is that there is a great deal of research going on about depression, and specialists are finding good treatments for it on both psychological and medical levels. If you suffer from depression, find a psychologist who has a good reputation in your area and interview him or her. It can be a step to a new life.

I have so much respect for the many people I have worked with who had that double burden of a tough life problem plus a depression. They shouldered the load and walked the steps. It was not easy, but they did the work, and I have seen wonderful results and fruit in their lives. They are an inspiration to me and to others in their lives.

## A Desire to Be Independent of God

This is not as much a psychological issue as it is a directly vertical, spiritual problem. There is a tendency in each one of us to go our own way, to provide our own answers, and to be independent of God. It is part of the sin nature. That tendency, resident within since Adam and Eve, resists our need to be dependent on Him as the Source for all the things we need: life, relationship, direction, strength, and wisdom. To some extent—mild, moderate, or severe— we would rather do things our way than His way. And when this tendency appears, we do not expect benefits from God even if it is clear that we need Him. This is because there is a disconnect for us in that state of mind. It is that if we were to see Him as providing help and comfort in our life troubles, it would mean we would have to admit our need to go to Him. This is a real trade-off. The Bible teaches it over and over. If we want Him to guide and protect us, we must be dependent on Him:

> But if you are careful to obey him, following all my instructions, then I will be an enemy to your enemies, and I will oppose those who oppose you (Ex. 23:22 NLT).

> Oh, that they would always have hearts like this, that they might fear me and obey all my commands! If they did, they and their descendants would prosper forever (Deut. 5:29 NLT).

> My child, never forget the things I have taught you. Store my commands in your heart. If you do this, you will live many years, and your life will be satisfying (Prov. 3:1–2 NLT).

> Jesus replied, "All who love me will do what I say. My Father will love them, and we will come and make our home with each of them" (John 14:23 NLT).

In business terms, it is a simple cost-benefit ratio. It costs our independence to receive His care. It's the best deal in history, but as a race, we continually walk away from it. We constantly end up in the bind of blinding ourselves to the good we can expect from Him so that we can have the illusion of not needing Him.

The only solution here, of course, is what the Bible calls *repentance*.

That is, we need to turn from our disconnect and return to Him. It takes humility and surrender, but it is the only way to expect what is available from a good God.

## IF YOU ARE HELPING SOMEONE WHO DOUBTS

You may not be doubting today. Instead, you may be in the position of being in a relationship with someone who is doubting if he can expect anything good from God in his life crisis. These days people are simply asking "God questions" a great deal. If that is the case, don't make the mistake of forgetting to listen to them. One of the problems Christians sometimes have is that we are so glad we have some answers, we are more involved in getting the answer to people before they have a chance to formulate a question. People with doubts need to know that someone else gets it and will not shoot a lot of theological ammo down their throats. You should allow time and several encounters to pass to make a connection that shows thoughtfulness and care: "The purposes of a man's heart are deep waters, but a man of understanding draws them out" (Prov. 20:5 NIV). I have found that when I am talking about God and His activity in hard times with someone who is exploring spiritual matters, the conversation will meander in many directions. This takes time. I used to feel some pressure to make sure I had every answer sewn up at every pass, but then I started thinking, *I don't think I'd like to be searching and talking to someone like me. I would feel too much like I was in a sales pitch and being boxed in.* So I gave all that to God, and now I try to connect with the person, answer some questions, and listen to what they are doing. That seems to be working better.

# CHAPTER 14

# NUTS AND BOLTS

When we encounter difficulty, sometimes it originates from a personal and relational problem rather than a philosophical question in our minds. So we go to God and ask for help. We want out of the problem. But as I mentioned in the first chapter of this book, the big picture of our spiritual growth is not an event but the development of the habit of relationship with God. What starts as a single meeting is designed to end as a lifelong connection. You already may be in some sort of a regular, habitual, and meaningful devotional time with God. You may have developed this discipline for decades as an integrated and meaningful part of your life. Or you may never have considered the thought or not even be familiar with the term *devotional*. Or you may talk to God in an exploratory fashion, simply driven by the circumstances you are now facing. It doesn't matter where you are at the time of this reading. What does matter is that you understand the value of looking at the nuts-and-bolts practicalities of what makes a relationship with God work for your good.

A life crisis is as good a time as any to start praying, reading the Bible, and seeking God. It often seems to be the thing people do when they are searching for answers in a situation that is out of their hands. However, things don't work right if all those habits simply go away when the crisis resolves. Something that was supposed to happen didn't happen—an attachment to God that becomes the center of your life, and that's pretty important. Instead, you simply searched for help, and that never transformed into a love relationship. Ultimately, God wants the connection. The power will always be important, but the presence will always be central to the way He designed us, for we are the temple of the living God. As God said:

> I will live in them
>> and walk among them.
> I will be their God,
>> and they will be my people.
> —2 Corinthians 6:16 (NLT)

For God, the highest value will always be the *living and walking* part. He is the Great Connector. It is what He has sought since the Creation: an ongoing, sustaining relationship of love and grace. A relationship built on 911 calls to Him is certainly a type of relationship, even a beginning of a relationship, but it is not the final destination.

I have had the experience as a psychologist of a person coming for therapy about depression or a destructive relational issue and attending only a few beginning sessions. In psychotherapy there tends to be a pretty rapid elevation of a person's mood in the early phase. This is because the individual feels relief that he is finally doing something about the problem and has some hope that the psychologist can help him even though the issue has not been dealt with at any depth. Though he has a way to go before the cure, he is encouraged by his initial connection with and trust in his psychologist. This tends to be an important juncture because sometimes the person will then decide he is fixed and leave the process. This is called *flight into health*. He flees the coming discomfort by wishful thinking and hopes that his good feelings will remain.

Sadly, the good feelings don't remain. When I have had this sort of situation, often the person will then call me back in a few months and want to enter treatment again. We'll talk, and I'll explain what I think happened and emphasize the need of doing this thoroughly and doing it right. Most of the time, the person will buckle down, face his fears, and finish the work of resolving the issue. I have heard of other therapists having the same person repeat the flight into health several times, hoping against hope that she would be better quickly. But that is not how real growth and change happen; it's an oven, requiring sustained time and focus, not several microwave sessions.

It is the same with God— He designed us for a lifetime of depending on and following Him in a relationship. We are better off developing a connection and a habit that is meaningful and sustaining.

## IS STRUCTURE A LOVE-KILLER?

Having said all this, I always have a little conflict when I think and write about spirituality and practicality. The two seem to be contradictory, or rather, it is more as if the good that comes from spirituality might be undone by practicality. Sometimes I think we expect the spiritual part of life to flow naturally and freely. Prayer should be something that happens and God shows up, so we want to take time to pray. Or reading the Bible becomes as natural as going online after work. Somehow talking about the *how* takes away from the magic of connecting with God. To clarify, when I refer to "time with God," I am not focusing on the concept of continual prayer and checking in with

God that is part of the spiritual life experience. That is an awareness and a way of life: "Never stop praying" (1 Thess. 5:17 NLT). Here, I'm talking more about the pattern of a set devotional period.

We can get caught up in the "shoulds" and "ought tos" of the spiritual life and quickly turn it to an empty and dreadful religious life filled with activities and checklists. We lose the heart of the matter, which is loving and connecting with God authentically in a real relationship. I know that if we go that route, the result will usually be a different sort of flight into health—once the marriage issue resolves, the sick person survives or passes away, or the financial issue turns a corner. It is a flight from living under the burdens of pleasing the law, rather than living under grace. And it is a relief to leave the world of empty religion. It does no good for us or for God, who has no interest in a series of meaningless external behaviors: "I hate your new moon celebrations and your annual festivals. They are a burden to me. I cannot stand them!" (Isa. 1:14 NLT).

We've already pointed out the problem of searching only for God's power and the problem of trying to maintain a useless list of performances that would keep God happy. But there is a strong reason for having a practical side of your spirituality; it is simply that the right structure enhances relationship.

Relationships require some amount of structure and arrangement to them. It doesn't have to be a lot, and it won't quench the emotional side of your relationship. The best human relationships have structure. Couples with kids get a sitter regularly for date night so they can have some time to chill and reconnect on a deeper level. Friends call to get coffee. People arrange small groups and parties at their homes. These plans aren't intimacy killers. Rather, they provide room, space, and time for love and closeness to grow.

We have neighbors who are great party people. They have perfected the art of making people feel at home, getting the right mix of individuals and interests, and having the right food and atmosphere. People are always bugging them to know when their next party will be. I always meet someone interesting at their events. Great relational moments happen in their home. But I also know how many hours of planning go on behind the scenes: menu development, invitations, grocery store trips, cleaning the house, and all the rest. Certainly people could have come together spontaneously; it happens. But it happens better when there is some arrangement involved.

I have other friends with whom I have more of a *whenever* relationship. We like each other and like to hang out together. But we really don't plan to get together; it's more of a last-minute text, asking, "Are you in town? Want to get lunch?" It's my fault as much as theirs. Our connections happen much less frequently than those for which we schedule our time together ahead of time. And it actually speaks to a deeper reality that these probably aren't the most sustaining and important relationships in my life. They aren't my Life Team though they are people I care about. On a spiritual level, I think it's the same. God is our Source of life. It is best for us to add some regularity to the connection and to go beyond whenever with Him. That is how the best relationships are deepened and grown.

In my own spiritual journey, I have learned a great deal about practicalities. I went through a long period of reading the Bible systematically, memorizing verses, meditating on them, praying, and fasting during my college days. However, I didn't deal with my own internal shoulds, and often I was afraid that I was letting God down if I didn't get a daily devotional done. So I was driven by a good deal of fear and performance-based religiosity. That wasn't all there was to it. At the same time, I still felt a love in my heart for God and a desire to get closer to Him. But my performance issues were like having a touch of the flu: you don't feel good, but you're not sick enough to stay home from work. The fear of letting Him down was always in the back of my mind. As I mentioned earlier, this is about the time I went through some teaching on what "abiding in Christ" meant, and that helped a great deal. I felt freer in my personal time with God.

I had a friend named Mark who freed me up, not on the spiritual level but on a being-normal level. I was in a weekly Bible study with him on campus. We used a small-group lesson plan that had assigned homework for us to do between meetings: write answers to questions about the Bible, journal experiences, and so on. Though I really got a lot out of the study, I was terrible at the homework part. I always got it done in about ten minutes before the study, just writing anything down so that it was completed. I felt like the loser of the group, the guy who wasn't really serious about his faith. I was serious; I just was a serious flake. But one day I was hanging out in Mark's dorm room the day of the study. About twenty minutes before time to walk to the study, he said, "Oops, time to do the homework." He whipped out his study guide, and I did, too, and we did it together. I was so relieved that I wasn't the only eleventh-hour crammer! His transparency helped me feel more normal, and it even helped me look at my own tendencies to compare myself with what I thought others were.

I have found that some people who have similar performance issues as the ones I have struggled with sometimes simply toss the structure part aside in order to be free of the experience of having to spend time with God. Their thinking is that they would rather wait and be open to those moments in which they truly, from a sincere heart, want to connect with Him. They eliminate the structure that they feel is getting in the way of a pure relationship. Though I understand that, I don't think it is necessary in order to make a more love-based connection. In fact, it would be a little like saying to your spouse, "I don't like the feelings of being obligated to our relationship. I want to feel free so that I can really desire a connection to you. I'll call you when I feel that, so until then, probably not." I have seen that happen in troubled marriages, and it does not end well at all. Unless there is some sort of severe problem going on that requires distance for healing, like abuse or infidelity, that could be destructive to a relationship. You can work through fear and performance issues without having to get rid of structure. You can rework your feelings toward God while not dropping your times with Him. This is because structure is not the problem; the heart is. Solve that, and you solve most of the rest.

## THE POWER OF CONFESSION

What does that mean in practical terms since this is the Nuts and Bolts chapter? It means that we are always better off spending personal time with God than not. Even if we are doing it wrong. Even if we are performance-based. Even if we are there to get only the Power and not the Presence. Even if we struggle with feelings of obligation and duty getting in the way of the relationship. Be honest with what you are bringing to the table. As the previous passage from Isaiah shows, the thing that God doesn't respond to is external worship with no heart. You are not present then, and He wants your presence—the good parts and the not-so-good parts.

Sometimes when a person is struggling with this concept, I suggest to him that maybe it's because he is not being honest with God. He may feel a little offended at that, but it is often true. When we drill down, we often find that what the person is really feeling is a host of negative emotions and resistances toward God: fear of His anger and disappointment, resentment that we *have to* spend time with Him, or disbelief that anything meaningful will happen as a result of our relationship, for example. And what I recommend is to bring the honest and negative feelings into the relationship with God. This is simply what the Bible calls *confession* or bringing truth to the relationship. If we confess the resistance and negatives, we are placing something that is broken and needs help into the lap of the One who wants to repair it for us. For example:

- God, I don't feel the time with You is truly beneficial to me in navigating my life and decisions; help me experience my dependency on You as my Source.
- God, I am still mad at You for my losses and failures; help me clarify what is going on so I can get through this and reconnect with You.
- God, I am afraid I will let You down if I don't do a devotional every day; help me see Your grace and desire for a relationship with me.
- God, I honestly would rather have Your power than Your presence; help me understand what a relationship with You is about.

Some of these issues may be a result of baggage that we dealt with in chapter 5: The God You Must Not Seek. And some are just life and the pressures we face in a world of hard times. Regardless, don't be put off by structure. Use it and the principles and ideas in this chapter to simply bring you to the table. When a measure of organization helps you show up with God, you will be better off.

## CONTENT AND PROCESS

If you have ever gone to a bookstore and browsed the religious section for devotional guides, you may have been overwhelmed. There are so many different ways to spend time with God. It's easy not to know where to start. Or for that matter, if you've been meeting with God for decades, it's hard to know where to go next. There is a way to look at this on a simpler level. All of these tools break down into two elements, and you can choose what best suits your agenda based on that. The elements are *content* and *process*. By *content* I mean the material, facts, and reality you are reading or studying: an arrangement of Bible passages, a one-year Bible, a study guide, or a devotional guide that incorporates Scripture with some thoughts about it. Content is just the information itself—the way that Scripture is presented in a helpful manner. You can read, listen to, or watch content on a video. We need to interact with content. It shows us reality: God's realities about Himself, the world, you, and your life situation. The realities can be principles, stories, prayers, instructions, and illustrations. Biblical truth can come in lots of forms.

*Process* refers to the more experiential and relational aspect of our connection with God: prayer, journaling, worship, and praise, for example. Process brings the heart in connection with the head. For people who have a hard time connecting to others, process is sometimes a little more difficult because we can't literally see God. But there is no substitute for process. It ties together your conversation and dialogue with God, your emotions, and your personal needs. Process was the missing link in my time with God. Once I just started talking to Him about my life and how I felt toward myself, others, my situation, and Him, and as I began to actually listen to Him, I entered a whole new world. I actually started looking forward to time alone with God. I was not only gaining truth lessons but also experiencing relationship at the same time. Then there are those resources that mix the two together, such as reading the Bible aloud in prayer, which can be a very powerful and growth-producing experience. (Henry Cloud's *Be Still* DVD is a great example of this.)

Content anchors you in reality; process keeps you connected on a personal level with God. Try different processes that change up the format for you. You may also find that one style needs to change as you change and mature over time as well. But this is about love and growth, and the more you can experience time with God as something you look forward to, something from which you draw life, the better. My seminary professor and mentor, Dr. Howard Hendricks, told us in class one day, "It is a crime to bore someone with the Word of God." He is right; it should be a felony! If devotional time is a bore, an intellectual exercise, or drudgery, dig in there and unearth the conflict.

## DEVOTIONS WHEN YOU ARE IN DIFFICULT TIMES

Scheduling and prioritizing personal time alone with God when you have tough times is not an easy thing. It is counterintuitive. But it is important. When creditors are calling you on the phone, the clock is ticking on your job search, you are exploring health alternatives because of a bad test result, or your marriage is floundering, common sense would dictate that you should take care of the crisis first. There are situations in which this is necessary, such as a firefighter dealing with a burning landscape, a soldier in a firefight, an ER surgeon working with gunshot wounds, or a single working mother with a very sick child and other kids to take care of—in other words, the emergencies of life. In those situations you need the help and support of other people to carry you through. However, in normal circumstances we are not in a total adrenaline-flushing state for an extremely long period of time. The body breaks down after too much time. We aren't built to be totally *on* at all moments in the day. So create the time and space, not to be on but to be connected and searching for God.

We live life in twenty-four-hour cycles: working, sleeping, relaxing, and connecting with others is generally measured by days. We think in terms of days: How my day went. What happened yesterday. How tomorrow is shaping up. It makes sense to look for God daily as well. But difficult times tend to get us off center, off our game. We begin to think in terms of the crisis. It defines us, our realities, and what is important. Our situations become the organizing principle in life. We develop habits of obsessing, worrying, and talking about the same things over and over again with no progress. A daily time with God breaks up the habits that are forming. It reconnects us with the Source of grace and help. And we gain perspective that we need: "I will praise you every day; yes, I will praise you forever" (Ps. 145:2 NLT).

There is also a psychological benefit to the daily meeting. It is the development of trust and confidence. Think of how hard it is to wrest yourself away from your crisis and go to the room or the place you pray. We all deal with catastrophes and our own needs for control and closure, but we make time to walk away from all that and spend a few minutes with God. And when the world does not end and you are still alive and you have been with Him, you know you can do this again. And again. And even more in the easier times. You are more confident that an ongoing relationship with God really can become the organizing principle of life.

In this discussion, I have also used the word *focus*. It is essential. Make the time 100 percent intentional on one thing and one thing only: being in God's presence. Focus makes all the difference in the world. The more you avoid all distractions and are intent on your relationship with God, the deeper you will go and the more you will experience Him, His grace, and His guidance for your difficulty. This is true in relationships in general. Focusing on the connection keeps couples in love. They make sure there is time to look at each other, listen to each other, and tell each other how they are feeling about life and their relationships. It also helps a parent stay in tune with her child. We have a rule at dinner: no cell phones at the table, no texting with the phone in your lap! When the kids are distracted, there is no connection; it's a relational fragmentation. Family time is precious enough as it is, so make the most of it. Focus makes a good friend into a great friend, the one you first think of when you are in distress. It maximizes the benefits of your time with God. Focus makes a difference in our career, success, performance, and achievements—though I hesitate to mention this aspect out of concern that your devotional time becomes less relational and more of an activity. But my point is that, in a multitasking world, it is vital to focus on a single task with God and yourself.

In the middle of hard times, focusing on relationship is not automatic. This capacity is developed over time. You have to eliminate the externals, such as phone, e-mail, Internet, and texting. Just shut them down for a while. For example, I used to try to have a devotional while driving to work. I actually thought I could do it, and sometimes, if I have to, I will. But in reality, I can't be 100 percent present. I am looking out for the loony in the next lane or trying not to be a loony. But you must also deal with the internals: anxiety, fatigue, your mind drifting, the to-do list for today, the "worries of this life" (Mark 4:19), including your present crisis. The voices in your head can be very loud. What do you do then? Try to stop thinking about them? Maybe, but in my experience it is like telling someone, "Don't think about a purple elephant." The focus involved in "don't think about that" often backfires. I recommend confession. Whatever is on the mental table, bring it to the relationship and get it out:

- God, I don't see a good job prospect on the horizon.
- God, I wonder if I am next in line to be laid off.
- God, I don't know if I will be able to pay my mortgage.
- God, I don't know if my medical condition will get worse.
- God, an important relationship is on the rocks and I am devastated.
- God, my child is out of control, and I am afraid for her welfare.

Put all that out first if that is filling up your head. Tell God your concerns and how you feel about them. Say to Him, "Let me leave all this with You. Help me know You are in charge and You will take care of me and mine. Bring me peace so that I can be with You." He will help you: "I trust in you, my God" (Ps. 25:2 NLT).

I have a friend who almost stopped praying because she was going through so many losses. She was experiencing several of the ones I just listed, all at one time. It was an extremely distressful and painful time for her, and it lasted for about a year. She had thought she simply had nothing to offer God in her prayer time and felt bad about it as if all she would do is complain and be a drain on Him (her theology of God's omnipotence has changed since then). But she really felt like she wasn't "doing devotionals right." It was a waste of God's time, she thought. Then, on top of all her circumstances, a close friend of hers died unexpectedly, and that was the breaking point. She simply gave up and said to God, "I have nothing to give you but my tears." And she literally spent her time with God weeping about the devastating turns her life had taken. Time after time, that is all that happened during her devotionals. She poured her sadness and losses out to God. Then within a few days, she read a verse that centered everything for her:

You keep track of all my sorrows.
> You have collected all my tears in your bottle.
> You have recorded each one in your book.
—Psalm 56:8 (NLT)

It was as if God had said, "Your tears are all you have, and that is OK. I will be with you in your tears." That was a turning point for her in her relationship with God and in how she spent her devotional time. She began experiencing these moments as a time that God welcomed her at her most broken points because His strength and care were there for her. It has been years since that experience, and she has never looked back.

# THE PSALMS IN YOUR DEVOTIONALS
# DURING HARD TIMES

For millennia, the Psalms are the place in the Bible where most people have first turned for help in times of trouble. They are real, raw, and emotional, and they point us to God and His provision. If you find yourself in the Psalms during these days, you will find God. There is no pretense, no making things nice for God's sake. There is reality, and you will be able to identify with the writer's pain. David, author of about half of the psalms, was a very real person with great strengths and great flaws. He was a man after God's own heart.

Scholars have categorized the Psalms into different types, and the largest category is the *lament psalms*. These are the ones that have to do with some very difficult situation that David or the other authors went through. The circumstance can range from personal suffering at the hands of others to national oppression. Most of the lament psalms have a strange organization to them: they start with a complaint and end with praise. However horrible the situation, the emotional tone—in almost every psalm—resolves into some form of hope and worship to God. For example, look at David's Psalm 13:

O LORD, how long will you forget me? Forever?
  How long will you look the other way?
How long must I struggle with anguish in my soul,
    with sorrow in my heart every day?
  How long will my enemy have the upper hand?
Turn and answer me, O LORD my God!
  Restore the sparkle to my eyes, or I will die.
Don't let my enemies gloat, saying, "We have defeated him!"
  Don't let them rejoice at my downfall.
But I trust in your unfailing love.

> I will rejoice because you have rescued me.
> I will sing to the LORD
>> because he is good to me (NLT).

If you read carefully, you see a sudden swing in David's mood: something happens between, "Don't let them rejoice at my downfall," and "But I trust in your unfailing love." What went on here? There is no evidence that the difficulty had been resolved. And David didn't have bipolar disorder, nor was he the kind of man who got nervous about his emotional protests. He didn't backtrack his raw feelings and say positive things in order to be "religiously correct."

This is important to understand because it can help you connect to God on a deeper level during your times of trouble. Many scholars think it is simply that David believes God has heard his plea and that he can now have hope that God will help. Think about this for a moment. David's circumstances have not changed, but his feelings have. He goes in desperate and comes out hopeful because God has heard him. It is the hearing—and David's faith that God has attended—that is the tipping point.

There is a psychological reality at play here that can be helpful to understand. In studies of infant-mother attachment, there is a capacity that good mothers have. It is called *containing*. The word refers to her ability to literally "take in" her baby's emotional distresses, thus calming him down. An infant is too undeveloped to understand emotions. As far as he is concerned, emotions are reality. If he is scared, he must be in horrible danger. If he is frustrated, the world is a very depriving place. If he is sad, his losses are bottomless. A baby can get into real trouble emotionally, with his feelings escalating to harmful levels of intensity if he has no help. It is impossible for him to self-soothe or use reason to calm himself the way adults do. He needs his mother to contain him.

A competent mother will simply hold her squalling baby and let him know she is there, rocking him, soothing him, and taking his bad feelings into herself. By doing this, she is modeling soothing for him to be able to do later. It is as if she is saying, "Look, your emotions are really strong. I know you are very unhappy and distressed, but I can handle your feelings. I can listen to them, and they don't scare me. I'll help you get through this." And in a few moments, the infant's respiration and pulse slow down; he becomes calm, and he is OK, stabilized again and reconnected to Mom and life.

I think the same principle is at play in these psalms of lament. David gives vent to his misery in intense and emotional language. He doesn't hold back. And God is there. God doesn't say, "You are so ungrateful, after all I've done for you," or "How selfish you are." Nor does He punish David for his attitude. He contains. God holds the protests and pain inside Himself; He collects each tear, each doubt, each hurt, each angry word. And David, being contained, feels heard, and as the scholars say, can now have hope in God. That is the miracle of the Psalms.

I have personally had the same experience with God, and perhaps you have too. Several years ago, I went through an extremely difficult period with a friend I had been close to. He and I got off track on a problem, and it quickly spiraled into alienation. No matter what I tried, especially in taking the beam out of my own eye and trying to own everything I could that I had contributed to our problem, nothing worked. Eventually the relationship ended, and badly. It was a horrible experience for me, one that was the subject of much lament-type prayer to God. I told him how bad I felt about the whole thing and how confused I was about the friendship ending. And every time I talked to God, it helped. I didn't become ecstatic or full of joy, nothing like that. But I knew He heard me, He understood my feelings, and He was for me. And my pain over the loss got a little better every time. He contained me, and eventually I was again able to praise Him for taking care of me. Nothing changed in the relationship. It has not been restored, and that is a sad memory for me. But something deep within me has gotten a lot better.

Look at all this from God's perspective. He has your life and your crisis in His grip. He is in charge of events. There are no surprises for Him, no train coming down the track. He holds the future, and He is making plans for your good. Your life may not be easy, but it will be good. All of that is settled in His mind. He wants these focused, relational moments with you so that He can be with you, care for you, grace you, and guide you in His ways. The last thing He wants is for you to pretend with Him, act as if it is all OK, see Him as a duty, be afraid of Him, or to avoid Him altogether. He wants all of you, even the anxious parts, so that He can continually stretch and strengthen your life and your perspective to something more closely approximating His viewpoint. The more contact you have with Him, the more opportunity you give Him to help you in your trouble.

I have to emphasize here that I hope you are not experiencing some sort of guilt message. That is the furthest thing from my intent. I have read and heard many of these claims when it comes to connecting daily with God:

- If He's really important, you'll show up.
- If you don't show up, it is a sign you aren't committed.
- Look at how much He's done for you; can't you spare a little time for Him?
- You need to discipline yourself to do this.
- The Bible says you are to do this.

There is some truth to some of these statements. The Bible does teach the importance of time with God, for example. But if we don't get beyond the reality that it is important and get to the connection with Him, this won't work. These sorts of messages used to motivate me for a week or two, but that was about it. Don't show up with God because you have to. Show up because He is good and you need Him, especially in these times.

One of the most truly spiritual people I know is a businessman named Tom. He is quite successful in his profession, and has been that way for many years. And he has also experienced very hard days: a highly dysfunctional upbringing in his family of origin, a serious drug problem in his past, a wife who has struggled with severe health issues, and kids who have gotten into trouble. But insofar as I am aware, and I have known him for many years, he never misses his time with God. Sometimes it is very emotional and full of painful conversation; sometimes it is celebration and worship; sometimes it is quiet and reflective. But when we talk about his relationship with God, there is never a *should* in his mind. For him, it is a desire. He not only needs God, he wants God. That is what it is about. Needing God is a universal fact and reality. Wanting God comes from the heart:

> O God, you are my God;
> I earnestly search for you.
> My soul thirsts for you;
> my whole body longs for you
> in this parched and weary land
> where there is no water.
> —Psalm 63:1 (NLT)

That is the attitude to develop, especially in hard times. Moments with God aren't about keeping Him happy or meeting His quota. They are for us, our sustenance . . . our very life.

# OTHERS IN THE ROOM

You will also find a great deal of help when you are with God and with people. We need time alone with Him and time together with Him. The early church devoted themselves together to prayer (Acts 2:42), and the same thing happens in church worship settings and small groups today. Small groups encourage intimacy and honesty with God. Some of my most important spiritual times have been within a small group setting. It is not easy to be vulnerable with God with others in the room. It is important to make sure the group is made up of people who are safe and full of grace and truth. My experience has been that the safer the people, the more real and transforming the experiences with God. It does not happen overnight, and it takes time to trust the group. Don't compare yourself to anyone in the group—the one who knows the Bible better or who seems to have the "best" prayers, whatever that means. God wants you, alone and with others. That is enough for Him.

# CONCLUSION

I n your own present-life struggle, there is an answer to the question, "Where is God?" It is that He has always been here, and He is here now. He loves you and is working actively for your good in His own way.

God has not left you twisting in the wind, nor is He playing hide-and-seek. He wants to be present with you and powerful for you in your circumstances. He may bring a miracle. He may create a new path. And He may walk with you through a loss. But however your hard time plays out, He is here.

One of the most helpful things we can do is to pay attention to those times when He may show up in some special or important way. That is our job, sort of keeping the scanner on for His words or activities. That is the essence of seeking the Lord. We are to stay tuned, so to speak, to "seek His face continually" (1 Chr. 16:11 NASB). God is on His own time schedule with us. He may want to let us know He is around when we least expect Him, so we should strive to stay continually aware of Him and open to Him. Our role is to seek and to seek continually. Here are some recommendations on paying attention.

# CHECK IN

It can be a helpful practice and habit to check in often with God. Since there is another reality that is invisible, it is easy to stay on the visible end of life's spectrum: work, relationships, and activities. Just as I addressed the value of breaking up the twenty-four-hour daily cycle with a devotional in chapter 14, you should break up the tyranny of the visible by simply taking a moment, several times a day, to look for any sign that God may be speaking to you. That is part of the *continually* that the Bible speaks of.

A way to approach this is to think of a human relationship you have that is very important to you in a positive and good way. This should be someone you care about deeply. It may be your spouse or a person you are dating seriously. It may be your child or a close friend or family member. You have most likely found yourself thinking about this person during the day. You wonder what he is doing, where he is, how he is feeling, what you'll be doing when you see him again. You don't have to force yourself to think about that person: "It is 11:30, time to think about my husband." Your mind simply ends up on him. Begin to think about God that way. He is thinking about you, and He has a great deal of grace and help for you. Simply be aware for the moment that it is God's universe, and check in. It may be a prayer, such as the one Eli taught the young boy Samuel: "Speak, LORD, for Thy servant is listening" (1 Sam. 3:9 NASB). Or it may simply be a question: *Is there anything going on that God wants me to see in this situation?*

Now that my wife and I are on the tail end of parenting with one son in college and one in high school, as I look over the past twenty years, I can say that my least favorite time was the junior high era. It wasn't bad by any means, especially when I compare it with other families who have gone through real nightmares. We actually had a pretty mild dose of attitude and behavior, and there were lots of good times with our boys. However, I simply enjoyed the other periods more: infancy, toddlerhood, primary school, and high school. Some parents love that time more than any of the others, and I thank God for junior high volunteers and pastors! But I remember talking to a couple of friends in similar situations back then. I had no plan in mind; I had just been praying and worrying. But I had truly been asking God where He was in our own difficult situation. In the end, three or four families rallied together to help our children get through those years in the most successful ways possible. We prayed together for our kids, came up with ideas and plans, and supported each other through the roller-coasters and the eventual more stable times. Those friends were a godsend to us, and we are still close today—parents and kids.

I believe those relationships were part of God's "showing up" for our family. I had tried to pay attention and check in to any answers He might have during that period, and I think they were the answer. This might not seem very spiritual and miraculous, but in my book, they qualified. The point is, check in often and look for God.

## BE OPEN TO GOD

We—in the human race—are in love with control. We like to have things our way in just about anything, from the presets in the car radio to what continent we live on, and we will do a great deal to maintain that. As I have mentioned, a difficult life situation clarifies what we actually do and don't have control over. And that is also how, in our dark days, we are to approach God. We cannot dictate how He will speak to us or convey something important to us. That is His way and His decision. So be open to God's voice and His communications to you. Bring your life problems to Him as you check in, and let Him know you are open to any way He leads, for you will follow.

Having said that, at the same time God has, through the ages, communicated Himself to His people in several predominant ways. People draw lines at different places here; I believe that God speaks primarily through the Bible, the Holy Spirit, other people, and our circumstances. In addition, I believe He also can and does speak through other means, such as a miraculous event, our dreams, or some manifestation of Himself. It is important to have a balance here, however, as it is easy to be confused as to what is from God, what is from our own desires or emotions, and what is from the devil himself. The check-and-balance is found in the Bible. Since Scripture is unchanging and trustworthy, we need to look at every experience through the lens of the Bible. Whatever doesn't fit into Scriptural teaching is ruled out: *God told me to rob a bank* doesn't work. However, even events that pass the filter of the Bible still need to be vetted by the mature people in our lives, the indwelling Spirit, and wisdom. A person who says, "I saw a map of New Zealand, and so God wants me to move my family there" needs a great deal of verification by other sources. This is not to put any sort of damper on the supernatural power of God. It has more to do with our using all of the sources of reality and truth that God has for us. It is what we do as we learn and grow in Christ.

Sometimes the connection may not be an answer for your current life problem, in a will-of-God way. He may simply be conveying that He is present and cares about you. When I was writing this book, I asked a group of mature Christian leaders how God has spoken to them personally in their own dark times of life. They provided some wonderful answers of experiences that made all the difference in the world on how their circumstances played out and how they were able to respond to both the situation and to God:

- a passage of Scripture that illuminated my situation
- an overwhelming sense of His grace and care for me
- a worship song that connected me with Him on a deep level
- a small group setting in which I could be safe and open to Him along with others
- being in nature and experiencing Him in His creation
- observing or creating art that had depth and meaning
- being with a spiritual director or mentor who helped me experience God with my head and heart
- an opportunity which opened a door in my life
- meditating on Gospel narratives which fleshed out the person of Jesus for me
- being still
- a personal loss which brought me to a deeper relationship with God
- learning to become emotionally present with God and myself in order to be open to Him
- words that made all the difference in what I was going through

This list could go on, but I included it to give you an idea of the many ways God connects. He will give us the resources. Our job is to listen for whatever way He will do that.

## HE KNOWS YOUR FRAME

Though we need to take responsibility to be open to any way God conveys Himself to us, realize also that He designed us and knows us intimately. He knows how we are wired and how best to reach us: "You made all the delicate, inner parts of my body and knit me together in my mother's womb" (Ps. 139:13 NLT). He wants to reach you. In educational psychology terms, some people are visual learners, some are auditory, and some are kinesthetic. You may find that there is a particularly meaningful and powerful way that you experience and draw close to God.

For many years, when I have asked people about the frequency of God's presence in their lives, for example, I have found a variety of answers. Some people said they feel God's closeness to them in a personal and experiential way at all times, 24/7. For some, it comes during worship or music or Scripture meditation times. For others, it is all about the daily devotional setting. For others, God is more present with them when they are in greater times of need. And for others, there is no rhyme or reason. I don't see a pattern in these responses at all. But what I do see is the reality that God is seeking out those who seek Him: "I love all who love me. Those who search will surely find me" (Prov. 8:17).

I am not one of those 24/7 people. I often feel very close to God in several of the forms mentioned above, and these are profoundly moving and growth-producing experiences for me. These experiences are very important to me in my relationship with God, but they don't occur during every waking moment. A lot of times I just go through life, relationships, work, and my activities like everyone does. I think about God pretty frequently during a work day, but I think about a lot of other things, too, and I can't think of everything at the same time!

I used to wonder if something was wrong with me, especially having several friends who report that continual presence experience, and these are stable, mature, biblically grounded people. I didn't know if I had some spiritual flaw or immaturity or character weakness that caused this. Then as I studied the subject over time, I realized that while we are continually to be seeking God as our Source, God gives us all what we need. He would not deprive us from some experience if we truly needed it. So my perspective is that I must not need this, at least not at this point in time. I always want to strive to know Him better and to grow in Him and to bear the fruit that He wants to bear in my life. We are all to continually follow, trust, and seek Him. And ultimately, the rest is up to Him: "And this same God who takes care of me will supply all your needs from his glorious riches, which have been given to us in Christ Jesus" (Phil. 4:19 NLT).

## WHERE IT ENDS UP

Finally, I hope that you have hope—real and substantive hope. In your own personal burden, the one that made you pick up this book, I hope you can see God working for you and for your good. You need two sorts of hope: hope for today and hope for tomorrow. For today, your hope is that He cares about you and will help when you call: "Call upon me in the day of trouble; I will deliver you, and you will honor me" (Ps. 50:15 NIV). You can find Him and His provision in the middle of your struggle, in the here and now.

And for tomorrow, there is our ultimate hope. It is based on the purchase Christ made through His death for those who have accepted His offer of salvation. There is a day coming; the date we do not know. But we do know that on that day, history will end as we experience it. On that day, God will be found and will reconcile the universe totally to Himself. All wounds will be healed, and all dark nights lifted:

> Then I saw a new heaven and a new earth, for the old heaven and the old earth had disappeared. And the sea was also gone. And I saw the holy city, the new Jerusalem, coming down from God out of heaven like a bride beautifully dressed for her husband.
>
> I heard a loud shout from the throne, saying, "Look, God's home is now among his people! He will live with them, and they will be his people. God himself will be with them. He will wipe every tear from their eyes, and there will be no more death or sorrow or crying or pain. All these things are gone forever."

And the one sitting on the throne said, "Look, I am making every-thing new!" And then he said to me, "Write this down, for what I tell you is trustworthy and true." And he also said, "It is finished! I am the Alpha and the Omega—the Beginning and the End. To all who are thirsty I will give freely from the springs of the water of life."
—Revelation 21:1–6 (NLT)

And on that day there is one question you will never need to ask again, and that is, "Where is God?" It will have been answered, once and for all. He will be continually ever-present with you—and you with Him—for eternity.

May God bless you, today and forever.

—Dr. John Townsend

# APPENDIX

## BOOKS ON GOD AND SUFFERING

A few of the best-known books dealing with the issue from a Christian and popular, nontechnical perspective are described here. C. S. Lewis wrote *The Problem of Pain* (New York: HarperOne, 1940) to "solve the intellectual problem raised by suffering" as well as *A Grief Observed* (New York: HarperOne, 1961) to deal with his deep sadness over his wife's death. Philip Yancey wrote *Where Is God When It Hurts?* (Grand Rapids: Zondervan Publishing, 1977) to explore the existence and meaning of pain. With physician Paul Brand, Yancey wrote *The Gift of Pain* (Grand Rapids: Zondervan Publishing, 1993) to explain some of the medical and spiritual functions of pain. He also wrote *Disappointment with God* (Grand Rapids: Zondervan Publishing, Kindle version, 1988) to deal with God's perspective and role in our losses in life. Psychologist Dr. James Dobson wrote *When God Doesn't Make Sense* (Carol Stream, Illinois: Tyndale Publishing, 1993) to bring hope to those who feel betrayed by God in difficult circumstances. *Suffering and the Sovereignty of God,* edited by John Piper and Justin

Taylor (Wheaton, Ill: Crossway Books, 2006), treats the issue with a theological emphasis on God's sovereignty. Timothy Keller's *The Reason for God* (New York: Dutton, 2008), an overall apologetic for Christianity, has a helpful chapter on the issue.

On a more broadly spiritual level, Rabbi Harold Kushner, after his son's death at age fourteen of a rare genetic illness, wrote the bestseller *When Bad Things Happen to Good People* (New York: Schocken Books, 1981). His conclusion was that God could not be both omnipotent and loving. Bart Ehrman, a biblical scholar, authored *God's Problem* (New York: HarperCollins, 2008, Kindle Edition). He concludes: "At the end of the day, I do have a biblical view of suffering" (locations 4814–21), but he is now an agnostic as a result of his study of the subject. Psychiatrist Viktor Frankl wrote *Man's Search for Meaning* (London: Masc. Hill, Kindle version, 1959) to describe his three years as a Jew in Nazi concentration camps and how he made sense of the experience. Nobel laureate Elie Wiesel's *Night* (New York: Hill and Wang, 1972) is an intensely personal description of his own concentration camp experiences.

# NOTES

## INTRODUCTION: WHERE IS GOD WHEN I NEED HIM?

1. David Biello, "Searching for God in the Brain," *Scientific American* (October 2007), www.scientificamerican.com/article.cfm?id=searching-for-god-in-the-brain&offset=5; Jeremy Hsu, "Scientists Locate 'God Spot' in Human Brain," FOXNews.com, SciTech, 10 March 2009, www.foxnews.com/story/0,2933,507605,00.html; and Uffe Schjodt, Hans Stodkilde-Jorgensen, Armin W. Geertz, and Andreas Roepstorff, "Rewarding Prayers," *Neuroscience Letters* 443 (2008): 165–8.

## CHAPTER 2: WHY ASK WHY?

1. Mark Larrimore, ed., *The Problem of Evil* (Malden, MA: Blackwell Publishing, 2001), xix.

## CHAPTER 4: FREEDOM IN THE SERVICE OF LOVE

1. John Townsend, *Loving People* (Nashville, TN: Thomas Nelson, 2008).

## CHAPTER 5: THE GOD YOU MUST NOT SEEK

1. John Townsend, *Hiding from Love* (Grand Rapids, MI: Zondervan, 1996), 29–44.

## CHAPTER 8: THE GOD WHO WORKS BEHIND THE SCENES

1. Bill Dallas and George Barna, *Lessons from San Quentin* (Carol Stream, IL: Tyndale, 2009).

## CHAPTER 9: THE GOD WHO TRANSFORMS YOU

1. Dr. Henry Cloud and I have written extensively on this concept in our book *Boundaries* (Grand Rapids, MI: Zondervan, 1992); Henry Cloud, *Changes that Heal* (Grand Rapids, MI: Zondervan, 2003).
2. Henry Cloud and John Townsend, *Raising Great Kids* (Grand Rapids, MI: Zondervan, 1999).

## CHAPTER 10: THE GOD WHO CONNECTS YOU WITH OTHERS

1. Dr. Henry Cloud and I have written about this more extensively in our book *How People Grow* (Grand Rapids, MI: Zondervan, 2001), "People Are God's Plan A."

## CHAPTER 11: THE GOD OF FAITH WHEN THERE ARE NO ANSWERS

1. C. S. Lewis, *The Screwtape Letters* © C. S. Lewis Pte. Ltd. 1942. Extract reprinted by permission.
2. Phillip Yancey, *Disappointment with God* (Grand Rapids: Zondervan, 1988), Kindle ed. 2358–66.

## CHAPTER 13: EXPECT THE GOOD

1. Mother Teresa and Brian Kolodiejchuk, *Come Be My Light* (New York: Doubleday, 2007), Kindle ed. 4334–42.
2. William J. Bouwsma, *John Calvin: A Sixteenth Century Portrait* (New York: Oxford University Press, 1998), 184.

# ABOUT THE AUTHOR

D r. John Townsend is a psychologist, author, speaker, and leadership coach who, for more than two decades, has been helping millions of people grow spiritually, emotionally, and relationally. Dr. Townsend is a visiting professor at Dallas Theological Seminary. In addition, he is an engaging and personable speaker, using a unique blend of wisdom, humor, and spirituality and offering keen insight on all aspects of life and growth.

A prolific writer, Dr. Townsend has authored or coauthored twenty books that have sold over five million copies, including the two-million-seller, Gold Medallion Award-winning book *Boundaries*. His latest book is *Leadership Beyond Reason*. His writing has earned him three Gold Medallion Awards as well as the Retailers Choice award.

Dr. Townsend is cohost of the nationally syndicated daily radio program *New Life Live!*, which broadcasts in more than 150 markets with three million listeners. Dr. Townsend has two television programs that air regularly on the Church Communication Network, and he has also appeared on FOX News, *Focus on the Family*, the Trinity

Broadcasting Network, and other media venues. Dr. Townsend conducts his own Leadership Coaching Program accelerating leadership and organizational performance, the Boundaries Boot Camp, and the Ultimate Leadership Workshop.

Dr. Townsend is also clinical director of the American Association of Christian Counselors. He serves on the board of directors of Mustard Seed Ranch and is also on the board of advisors for two other ministries: India Gospel League and MOPS (Mothers of Preschoolers).

A North Carolina native, Dr. Townsend earned his bachelor of arts degree in psychology at North Carolina State University. He went on to obtain his master of theology degree from Dallas Theological Seminary and a MA and PhD in clinical psychology from Biola University in California. He, his wife, and their two sons reside in Southern California.

Contact information:
www.drtownsend.com
www.cloudtownsend.com
townsend@drtownsend.com
800-676-HOPE (4673)
949-249-2398

# Ultimate Leadership

## The Ultimate Leadership Workshop

**The Ultimate Leadership Workshop** is a highly effective weeklong training retreat developed and taught by Dr. Henry Cloud and Dr. John Townsend to accelerate professional and personal growth. The Workshop is geared toward anyone whose work influences the lives of others. Based on biblical principles of leadership and character development, this intensive program has been proven to achieve significant gains in performance and in life. You will learn new and powerful ways to attain professional and relational success. The Ultimate Leadership Workshop is a breakthrough experience to help you reach the next level.

To view Drs. Cloud and Townsend discussing the benefits of the Ultimate Leadership Workshop, go to **drtownsend.com/ulw**

# Boundaries

## BOOT CAMP

**Boundaries Boot Camp** is a weekend experience developed and presented by Dr. Henry Cloud and Dr. John Townsend, authors of the two million-seller Gold Medallion Award- winning book Boundaries. Get hands-on training with the boundaries experts themselves. Boundaries affect every relational area, and even habits like overeating or procrastination. Boot Camp will help you get fit from the inside out. Learn to apply good boundaries with family, friends, co-workers and even bosses. Not only will you see the benefit of confronting tough situations, you will take the next step to achieving solid boundary-setting skills. You will leave the workshop with the ability to put the principles you've learned into practice.

For more information about Ultimate Leadership or Boundaries Boot Camp, please visit our website at www.cloudtownsend.com; email ct@cloudtownsend.com; or call Cloud-Townsend Resources at 800-676-HOPE (4673).

To view Dr. Townsend discussing the Boundaries Boot Camp, go to drtownsend.com/bbc.